© Silvie Byng

Holly Dawson is a writer, editor and teacher. Since 2018, she has been Reader-in-Residence at Charleston, where she gets to indulge her passion for Modernist literature and Virginia Woolf. Her plays, drawing on Bloomsbury diaries and letters, have been performed by actors including Helena Bonham Carter, Miranda Richardson and Jonathan Pryce. Having grown up in Cornwall, she now lives in rural Sussex with far too many hens.

@hollyjdawson | hollyjdawson.com

All Of Us Atoms

HOLLY DAWSON

CANONGATE

First published in Great Britain in 2025
by Canongate Books Ltd, 14 High Street, Edinburgh EH1 1TE

canongate.co.uk

1

British Library Cataloguing-in-Publication Data
A catalogue record for this book is available on
request from the British Library

ISBN 978 1 80530 147 9

Typeset in Van Dijck by Palimpsest Book Production Ltd,
Falkirk, Stirlingshire

Printed and bound by CPI Group (UK) Ltd, Croydon CR0 4YY

For those who have gone
and those who will go

And, what is this moment in time, this particular day in which I have found myself caught? [. . .] Time has whizzed back an inch or two on its reel; our short progress has been cancelled. [. . .] our bodies are in truth naked. We are only lightly covered with buttoned cloth; and beneath these pavements are shells, bones and silence.

— Virginia Woolf

I am an instrument in the shape
of a woman trying to translate pulsations
into images   for the relief of the body
and the reconstruction of the mind.

— Adrienne Rich

I am who I am, doing what I came to do, acting upon you like a drug or a chisel to remind you of your me-ness, as I discover you in myself.

— Audre Lorde

If we had a keen vision and feeling of all ordinary human life, it would be like hearing the grass grow and the squirrel's heart beat, and we should die of that roar which lies on the other side of silence.

— George Eliot

I want to seize my is.

— Clarice Lispector

This Much Is True

All of us dream. But we do not dream equally.

When we have power, our dreams let us visualise: everything we want; we will achieve; we will be.

When we do not have power, we must fantasise. Our fantasies bring hope, compensation, relief.

When we have power, we need only know one thing: the linear mechanisms of the advancement of ourselves.

When we do not have power, we need to know everything: the riddle of Otherhood, of the Unlived Life.

When we do not have power, we gain Imagination. We understand everything. We are part of a whole.

The Powerless thus hold their own power: the imagination necessary to solve, and survive.

You can take our voices. You can take our bodies. You can take it all, everything. But this much is true: there is a secret place inside us you can never hope to conquer, to claim, to control.

This Much Is True

Contents

I Think Therefore I—

So you're forgetting things. So what? So you walk into a room, blank, walk out again, get a plate out, blank, put it back, turn the taps on, blank, flood the bathroom. So faces appear without names, so you freeze at the checkout, stuck on your PIN.

So what? It's funny. Till it's not.

Because now you're mm-mi-madd-muddling your words, and it's not funny, how they slip when you summon them, how you flail about in their loss. It's not funny, still trying to grasp them hours later from the syllable or signal they left behind. And it's not funny when you're teaching, dancing around the whiteboard, and suddenly – what was I—where was I going with—what's the name of—so—I was going to say—what?

So this – a consultant, opening a test book, making space between you on a chaotic desk. She apologises for her temporary office. You hope she means an office for diagnosing temporary things.

They had warned you this might happen. Best-case scenario, it's a side-effect of your meds. Else it's the start of our time together running out. Except it can't be, you're not even forty. The world is still for getting, not forgetting.

Hold tight, my girl. We've never failed yet.

Okay, Holly, the consultant says. I'm going to read out twenty words. When I'm finished you will say as many as you can back to me:

Market   Package   Bubble

She shouldn't have called you Holly. This is my test, not yours.

Apple   Pumpkin   Saddle

Fourteen more, then our turn. You start confident and fast:

Market   Package   Apple

Missed one. Don't look at her. Close your eyes. Find me.

B . . .

Sorry, you say to her. B . . . Burr . . . *Bubble*

We did it! Keep going. The next three are fine. Then –

Ess . . . Ssss . . .

The *S* shimmers large then bolts from you, leaving behind brown leather, a shape.

Satchel?

Not quite, Holly. *Saddle.* Carry on.

You fumble about for more of them. We don't make it to the end of the list.

Don't be cross with me, my love. I am tired. It is so tiring, being your brain. Between your ears hearing a word and your mouth repeating it, I am doing all this work you don't see. The doctors know this work, because they see me as your Body. But you see me as your Mind. I am *you.* You are *me.*

Okay, Holly. Second exercise. I'd like you to look at the image on this page. After ten seconds, I will turn the paper over and you will draw what you remember. Okay?

She shows you eight pictures. Random assemblies of dots, shapes, lines. You manage four toddlerish approximations. You remember being criticised at nursery for not keeping your crayon inside the lines.

Sorry, you say to the woman, as if it's a moral responsibility to replicate how triangles collide.

Do you need a break, she asks.

No, you say.

But I need a break. You didn't ask *me*.

When you were born, I wasn't sure I got the best deal. I wasn't too thrilled with half your genes. But oh, your women. They saved me. Saved us. Your mother, your auntie, your gran.

Three, and we could already read. Four, and we had a little desk of our own. Our women always talking to us, reading, taking us to the library, scouring jumble sales for books. Food could be short, but their stories were long, and they poured their knowledge into us like we'd never get full up.

Five, we were too clever for school. We skipped a year. You were tiny, I was huge.

Six or seven, we could recite reams of poetry, and began spooling out notebooks of our own. Eight, and we memorised Shakespeare. Wrote our first novel aged ten.

Eleven, we began keeping a diary. You and I, together, making sense of the world. Thirty years and a hundred or so volumes later, we still do it. It's the longest relationship you've ever had. What began as a courtship — sparkful, intimate — grew into a marriage that keeps us safe, makes us strong.

How lucky I was to be born to you. But you have pushed me too hard, for too long.

Okay, Holly. Take a look at these numbers. I want you
to remember them, and then say them to me, but
backwards.

Cognitive Crufts. Woof! Woof! Come on, that was funny. When
did I stop making you laugh.

7. 5. 2. 9.

See? I got it right. We can do this.

8. 0. 3. 6. 9 – was it 6? – No – wait – 5.

8. 0. 3. 5. 9 . . .

Why are you letting me down, you shout at me.

When did you stop trusting me, I shout back.

Okay Holly. We're halfway through. Get some water,
stretch your legs.

You lock yourself in the toilet and cry. Are you crying for me,
or for you, or for us both?

You go back to the room before you are ready, because you don't
like people thinking anything's wrong.

Look at these words, Holly. They are the names of
colours. But not the colour they are printed in. So

this word says 'Blue' but it's printed in red. I'd like you to go through the list only saying the printed colour. Does that make sense?

Not really . . .

She explains it to us again. Our turn.

Blue. Red. Red. Green.

Two reds in a row? Can't be right. Go back.

I want to tell you: it isn't my fault we are here. I have been trying my best for you all your life. I had no choice but to make it physical. I knew you'd only notice me if I took away your words.

I am like that old woman screaming HELP ME on the trolley, so close to you that her foot was on your sheet, and you saw it was pussing and purple, and she wouldn't stop screaming, but nobody came.

Peak pandemic, A&E shrunk to one corridor, nurses moving trolleys like a jigsaw they couldn't solve. They jolted your trolley a few inches and squeezed a chair into the gap for a woman to sit down. She was young, and moaning, clutching her stomach.

Ectopic pregnancy, the paramedic told the nurse.

You looked at the young woman losing her baby. You wanted to hold her hand, but touch was not allowed.

You have always felt other people's pain. I knew if I wore my pain on the outside, you'd pay attention to me too.

So I had no choice. I created your first full tonic-clonic seizure.

She's shaking, someone shouted.

I knocked you out. You woke up in a room and your first words to the doctor were *I'm sorry, I'm sorry, I'm fine.*

But me? I was not fine. This was my show now. So I drenched you in sweat and sent you spasming again.

When you came to, you were in a white tunnel.

Hello, I said to the scanner. Look at me. I'm here.

The consultant returns to the market/apple list.

So Holly, how many can you remember now?

When you'd arrived at the appointment, you had babbled out a caveat:

Before we start, I guess it's marked on averages, and
I just need you to know that what might be average
is not average for me. Like, if an Olympic runner

7

turned up to a community track, people would be like Wow he's fast, but the runner would see how much slower he ran than usual and know that he had massively failed.

Okay, Holly. That's fine.

I don't know if that makes sense, but I mean, words are my thing, so even if I mess up a little bit, for other people it might be normal, but for me that's really bad.

That's fine, Holly.

So the scores might show I'm fine, but I need you to know I'm not. I'm not.

That's fine Holly. I'll put it in your notes. Let's start.

There's a clever-tongued man you like sparring with because he outsmarts you, which is rare, and a thrill. Conversations with him — competitive, combative, collegiate — always act as catalysts for new ideas, new thoughts. We like men who teach us. If things had been different, that's what a father would have done.

You tell the clever-tongued man about your failing memory, the way an athlete admits an injury before a race. You want him to tell you something profound, something consoling. Something to make this all start to make sense.

You're drinking from the wrong cup, he says.

You lower your mug of black coffee. He laughs and shakes his head.

Mnemosyne, he says. That's whose cup you need.

He tells you the Mother of the Earth had twelve children and the greatest was Mnemosyne, goddess of memory and inventor of words.

And Time too, he adds.

Three gifts, co-dependent, that create and sustain each other: language, memory, time.

She's perfect for you, he says.

Not any more, you reply.

He tells you Mnemosyne also had another job. When souls died, they had a choice: drink from the River Lethe to forget their lives, or drink from Mnemosyne's pool to remember them.

So if this was Ancient Greece, he says, you'd go to the temple, not the neurologist, and you'd have two drinks – first, a chalice of Lethe-water to empty yourself of every thought you'd ever had. Then you'd drink the water of Mnemosyne, and all the thoughts you'd ever had would rush back in. Then the priest would sit you on the Chair of Memory and you'd have to garble back everything you have learnt.

That would be more fun than scalp electrodes, you reply.

No, he says. It puts your soul in a state of terror and panic till you pass out.

Well, I know all about that.

He looks at you with pity, which is why you don't tell people this stuff.

Your family lift you off the chair, he continues. They hold you until you come round. In the days after the ritual, you recover.

How do you know when you're cured, you ask.

When you regain the power to laugh.

You go quiet, then, because you understand it, and you don't think it will end with a laugh.

Hospital for you has always been the Lethe chalice. When you lay in that white tunnel the first time, you let go. Enjoyed the blankness. Found rest. I did too.

My love, if you had listened to me, we could have found that rest together all along.

The scan showed calcification. We have turned ourselves to stone. There was also a tumour.

> Likely benign, said the doctor. You've probably been living with it for years.

> Will I die?

He'd shrugged his shoulders.

> Something else will kill you before that.

I didn't like his nonchalance. I didn't like being dismissed. I had to keep making it worse for you. So the seizures kept coming, and they kept putting you on new drugs. And you kept on going, like everything was fine.

So I'm sorry. I'm sorry. But everything wasn't fine. I had no choice but to take away your words.

> It seems so unfair, you said to another friend. My brain is all I've got.

> She said, You've got more brains than all of us put together. A little bit going wrong won't be too bad.

> I had to put a Post-it note on the coffee machine to remember how it works. Coffee for Christ's sake. I make it every day.

11

Oh, I always forget things – that's what people often say to you. It's just life! Or peri-menopause! Or stress!

No, it is not those things. Unless 'just life' leaves you convulsing on the sofa, your children calmly waiting for you to come round, putting a straw to your lips because they know you'll wake thirsty, covering you with a blanket because they know you'll be cold.

The children have noticed how muddled your words get. It has become a running joke.

> Make yourself a seatbelt.
> (Giggle) Do you mean crumpet?

> Put teeth on your pyjamas.
> (Oh how they laugh and do just that)

When your eldest saw the Post-it note on the coffee machine, he thought the instructions were for him. He woke you up with a hot cup wobbling precariously.

> Did I do it right? he said.

With every new diagnosis, new drug, you update the emergency instructions on the fridge. In red pen it says 'Mummy has epilepsy'. The new consultant thinks you've had it all your life. There are over thirty types of seizures, not just the fitting you see on films. Your episodes had gone ignored, written off as something else: mental health, overworking, hormones, fatigue.

You tell the boys – because curiosity soothes them –

Did you know Valentine was the saint of epilepsy, not just love?

The final test should be the easiest. It involves a short story. That's our thing! The consultant reads it aloud. It's boring. Every sentence crammed with locations, facts and names. Call this a story? we want to correct her.

Still – we've got this.

We've got this, right?

No. What's happening. What was – where was –

No, we can't tell her the name of the hotel or how many fire-fighters came when it burned down.

No, we can't repeat it word for word back again.

No.

We haven't got this at all.

You lie your head on the consultant's desk. I curl up in your cranium and make you cry.

I am giving up these tests now. I'm tired. We have been in this room for an hour and a half. I want you to go and hide in the toilets. I want you to find my hurt in your hurt.

Last test. No, I can't join these dots in a sequence. I'm exhausted from joining the dots together all your life.

Do you remember when you were little, how travel-sick you used to get? Every car, bus, coach journey had you sitting by the window with a bowl on your lap. The adults tried everything. Windows down, no reading, a tiny tablet that tasted of salt. The mantra: Keep looking straight ahead.

Do you remember how they explained it to you, that travel sickness? The confusion between your Body and your Brain. Your ears and eyes saying: We're moving! Your muscles saying: No we're not! And me in the middle, refereeing. Conflicting signals. Are we moving? Are we not?

They told you, Being sick is like your brain and body having an argument.

I was giving you a warning, even then.

I love you, my girl. But I was always second to your Body.

I know how long you have hated your Body. But why didn't you see? Every time you hurt it, you hurt me too. You say: Stop eating. Your hungry Body obeys. You say: Keep dancing. Your broken Body twirls on. You say: Run a marathon. It does it. Don't sleep! Work all night! Birth these babies! Build this thing!

How servile your skin is. How you bend it to your will. But it is turning on you now. You're afraid I'll turn on you too.

People always saying –

I don't know how you do all this!

I'm like Thatcher, you joke. I don't need to sleep.

But I did, my love. I needed rest. Instead, behind your smile, you'd hiss at me, Come on! Stay awake! Keep achieving! Keep going! Don't dare stop.

And now we are here, my girl. And I'm tired. And you're tired too, I think.

The results of the memory tests destroy you. The first time you've failed anything.

Not now. Not this.

For each task, you are 'borderline' or 'below average'. For one exercise 'extremely low average'. You didn't need to give her the spiel.

You read the results twice, underlining the important bits. You don't tell anyone. You feel ashamed.

But something happened for us, when we read them. You felt me. When you were crying, it was for us both.

I'm sorry, you said to me.

I'm sorry too.

This is going to get worse, isn't it, you said to me. What if we run out of time.

Death and memory are linguistic bedfellows: remembrance, memorial, in memoriam. 'Mourn' from *murnan*, root *mer*, to remember. *Damnatio memoriae*: expunged from history, erased from official accounts.

Sometimes, they talk about cutting me open. They call it a Last Resort. Epilepsy never gets better, they said, it just stays the same or gets worse.

You research craniotomy. It doesn't make you afraid. You wouldn't mind them doing it, if it would get me to shut up. If they could separate me from your Body again and I could go back to being your Mind.

Let them do it then, if they will. They will find a temporal lobe blasted with holes. They will find the ashes of my sizzled hippocampus. They will cut away the stone, and the bits that went wrong.

Cut me open, and soldiers will sing Latin as they carry and kiss their dead.

Cut me open, and a library will fly out of us, and pages from the books left unwritten in your head. Every letter we've received, every diary we've confessed to, every notebook filled by your grandmother's hand. Out they'll fly, flocks of words, said and unsaid, sung and unsung, dictionaries murmurating in French and Latin, Cornish and Greek.

Take your scalpel to us and unfurl the ribbons. Unweave these truths, untruths, half-truths.

I can't promise we will have that much time, my love. But I have left something for you, when I fail.

I took the best parts of me and made your boys. The left side I bestowed on your firstborn: facts, knowledge, lists. The right side of me grew into your youngest. The poetry, the brush-strokes, the dance.

These are the gifts I will leave you. Even I, like you, must grow old.

One day, my love, I will leave you. We both know that. Hard as it is.

Until then, I'm here. Notice me. Heal me. Accept that I am part of a whole. Know that there is nothing but dark silk between us, between your Body and your Mind.

When it's time, you mustn't fear letting go of me. But there's something we can do before then.

Come.

Sit.

Take your notebook. This page is the bridge between your Body and your Mind.

Write it down. Write out all of it. Drink Mnemosyne's liquor, and I will roll out these stones.

Write, and we will toss them like bones and see what stories are told where they land.

The Memory

There's a memory you hold on to, like you're saving it from a fire, or a flood.

No special event. Nothing to photograph. Just beans on toast with your gran. You were seven years old. It was autumn. You'd just finished watching a film.

The Memory spans about thirty minutes. But that half hour dilated. Sucked you treacle-like in. Time was a hole you fell into, and when you climbed out again, you were changed.

You want to preserve this memory. You're the only one left who can. Where to start? With the beans on toast perhaps. Or the film you were watching before. Or the years leading up to it – your years, your gran's years. To Shakespeare. To a tired king, six centuries before.

But no. You can't open the Memory. Lift the lid and you'll lose its light.

Start with this then: the setting for that memory. A stage is appropriate, after all.

Your gran's house looked normal from the outside – a pebbledash semi, on a post-war estate. The streets were all named after Viking words, jumbles of consonants that gutteralled your tongue. You giggled as you tried to pronounce them, as she told you the origin of each. Her road was named after the waterway that connected three countries to the sea, so you didn't walk to her house, you rowed there, commanding your longboat through the waves.

A house from the outside – but inside, a library, a gallery, museum. Books, so many, floor to ceiling, on shelves, on tables, on rush-weave chairs. Everywhere crammed full of treasure. Ornaments and objects, pictures and plants. Colourful blankets, tapestry cushions, curtains with patterns of birds. The brown swirly carpet with hessian rugs on it, like a path through a forest floor. The kind of house you'd expect to find cats in, but she was allergic, so had rabbits instead.

You loved this house, because you loved your grandmother, and the house was like being inside her great big mind. You were allowed to touch everything, read everything, ask everything, as if she'd put it all there for you to explore. No order, no rules. A fun house. You always left bigger than when you'd arrived.

There was a particular smell in your gran's house. Even now, you can't pin it down. A smell that bundled all of her together – her hairspray, her cooking, her dewberry soap. Butter and gravy, lavender and dust.

Her house was always warm, like she was. Everything that made heat in her home glowed blue – the stove, the Calor gas heater – so that the warmth you shared with her seemed blue to you, and the Memory, this particular memory, appears through a blue-tinted haze.

But no. Go back. Zoom out. There is so much more to say.

When you were little, you were often with your grandmother, and nothing was dark, or broken, or hard. She was a warm, wide lap to climb into, and a cloud of white hair, and bright silk scarves. She called you *Treasure* or *Poddle*. You had secret codes, your own sayings and routines, and she drew diagrams of everything you wanted explained, and wrote down long words that were new. She told stories about the antics of your mum and auntie and your uncles when they were kids – although it was impossible to you that she could have been a mother, just as your mother could never have been young.

She was a big woman, whose life should have been bigger. In the end, she was so small.

An only child, she was actually a second child, growing in the shadow of a brother dead at birth. Should have been a boy – she often said that. She was close to her father and had a twinkle in her eye. Still, she'd be a *lady*, hoped her shopkeeper parents, who set about striving for her to become *middle-class*. Convent school,

21

Latin, good posture, and a place won at Cambridge (says the story, true or not).

Her father liked to take her to the golf course. She was a small white ball, poised precisely on a tee, waiting for the touch of a sophisticated gentleman to swing her up into the world. Instead, she was picked up by the ball-boy. A scallywag, scrumper, dashing but uneducated, one of nine siblings, charming of course.

Bride at nineteen. Mother five months later.

She lost all her teeth to quick pregnancies and had false ones you liked to watch her take out. Her hair turned pure white in her twenties. Four children later, she was poor and divorced.

Poor and divorced – but free. And busy, every minute of the day. She drank from the life that she should have had when her real life left her parched.

No official degree, but a clutch of first-class honours from a cottage university all of her own. She devoured books, sought knowledge, information. Libraries, evening classes, talks. Radio Four providing the curriculum. Newspapers, like a common room, colouring the gaps.

What would she have studied at Cambridge? Archaeology, you're sure she once said. Instead, she became the family archaeologist, storing and labelling every artefact she dug.

She kept everything. Every notelet, every postcard, every ticket stub, every toddler's clumsy maquette. Hundreds of photo albums. Items of clothing. Video tapes, cassette tapes, collections of stamps. Objects with meaning. Souvenirs. Furniture.

If something held a story, she kept it. And stories can be found in most things.

When a baby was born, she bought that day's newspaper, kept for posterity in a folder with their name. Smuggled a Dictaphone in her handbag to family gatherings to preserve conversations, uncensored, banal. Her Filofax diary held the dullest of secrets – lists of birthday presents gifted and received, family dress sizes, international cricket scores, bullet-point summaries of each day's soaps.

This was where history came alive for her, in the humdrum minutiae of ordinary things. By writing absolutely everything down, she was curating a future that would marvel in the mundane.

As custodian of the past, and archivist of the present, she could edit what versions of stories passed on. Everything she knew, she poured into you, and everything she didn't know, together you made up. Such is the art of the imaginative historian. She told her stories until they were true. You lived together in an Other Place, half-real, half-invented, part-present, part-past.

Four, and she taught you to puff your chest out and pretend to be Elizabeth I, proclaiming to your armada of boating-lake pedal-boats: *I know I have the body of a weak and feeble woman, but I have the heart, and the stomach, of a king!*

Six, and you joined her adult history group, touring castles and museums, followed by Wednesdays, when your mother went to Psychology evening class, and you tiptoed out of bed for history lessons downstairs. In summer, she took you to work with her, and you were free to roam the castle while she gave guided tours.

She was always most present in the past. And now she's in the past, she is always still present.

You need to remember all this, before facing it. To remember Time is a dance, not a march. That there are no lines, with beginning and end points, just circles upon circles, within loops, twists, swirls.

This is the Memory: a distillation of those circles.

This is the Memory: beans on toast, bleeding noblemen, and *non nobis domine*, sung by the stove.

Start with the song, then. With *non nobis domine*.

Hear it, now. Allow a low hum. Let it start quietly, as if happening in the distance. You, on her lap, in her Viking sea home.

You, on her lap, cuddling up in knitted blankets. For two hours and twenty minutes, neither of you have moved. On the TV in front of you, the end of a battle. As the dead lie dying, a peace of sorts falls.

Men – but not as you know them. Noble, tender, and calm. Henry, the king, but not king-like, blood on his face, on the lions on his shirt. Weary. Not afraid to show weariness. Humble and solemn, despite winning. Not proud.

Eloquent, these men, such poetry, an elegiac otherness flowing from their tongues.

You don't need to grasp the strange language to cry for them. Both of you crying, cuddled up on the couch. Sobbing, but silent, because you don't want to miss anything. Armour jangles, as they carry their dead.

The king lifts poor Robin – the boy, barely older than you – Robin the porter-boy, that's all he was – slung over King Henry's shoulder, limp and leaden and dead. As young as you and dead, and it's wrong, and the king – you can tell – he knows it's wrong, like you. He doesn't have to say anything, you just know it, like you're reading his mind, like he's you on the screen.

As the sad king walks through the battlefield, a soldier starts singing in a language you don't know. He keeps on singing, as the king keeps walking, through the living and half-living, the dead and soon to be dead. Through mud and blood and spent arrows. The voice still singing, and others joining in – *non nobis domine, sed nomini, sed nomini* – round and round, this looping lament.

On the king walks, the boy getting heavier, the king getting heavier as he takes it all in – the destruction, the waste, the wreckage. His heaviness makes you heavy too.

On he goes, taking Robin to his resting place, to the cart with the bodies piled high. He lays the boy down with such tenderness. Then leans over him closely, and kisses his head.

So this is what death is like. Carry them. Hold them. Sing to them softly. Kiss their heads.

The credits start rolling. Your gran wipes her eyes, squeezes you closely, and goes off to the kitchen to make lunch.

She can shift between worlds, but you can't yet. You're stuck there. Everything, and nothing, is the same.

The clock stops ticking.

You have fallen. Where are you?

Everywhere and nowhere. Not here – but here.

You're seven, and it's 1990 – but it's also Agincourt, it's 1415.

You're you, but you're also poor Robin. You're also King Henry, who didn't want to be king. You're the soldiers, half dead but still singing. You're even the horses, gone blinded and lame. You're the women who wept over their husbands, you're the villagers in aprons clinging to their sons – and you're also your gran, who had cried just like you'd cried, you had sat there together and you had felt the same thing – and –

– and when you feel the same thing with a person, *you become them*.

The discovery, overwhelming, rips a hole in the universe. Everything you ever knew splinters apart – your body, your thoughts, the TV, the living room, the minutes, the years, the this-is-this, that-is-that – all of it, shredded and flying around – even words, so dependable, even words just dissolve – and you're there in a hole, you can't put it all together again, everything that was solid before is now air – and why didn't they tell you – does everybody get this – your heart is a hundred hearts tightening in your chest – why didn't they tell you, why didn't anyone tell you, that you can be so many people *at the same time* as being you.

How frightening, how beautiful, to be everyone. How thin the silk separating you safe from the whole.

Your gran doesn't know this is happening. She's busy in the kitchen, not stuck down a hole.

She had felt what you'd felt when the film was on. But when it was over, she was fine straight away. Like you'd been on a train together, and she'd stepped onto the platform and left you hurtling alone on board.

She is normal again, making lunch in the kitchen. You try, like a rope, to hold on to her sounds. The tin, tapping into the saucepan. The clank as she pulls out the grill. The bread knife, slicing the granary. Her voice singing *non nobis domine*, soft and low.

Maybe you'd feel better if you understood the language. If you were as clever as your gran, who never falls down holes.

Knowledge. That's the way out of this. When you know things, they cannot dissolve.

It has taken a long time to interrogate this memory. For thirty years – longer – you kept the lid shut. Would it have helped, to have spoken about it with her? No. She didn't know. She was happy making lunch.

She might have remembered the conversation you had afterwards, as you ate beans on toast, butter dripping down your chin. She liked to boast to her friends about your cleverness. The stories of what you did together confirmed her intellect. Making out you were extraordinary made her extraordinary too.

For her, perhaps, this was the story – something she'd have told her friends:

I had my granddaughter on Saturday, and do you know, that little Poddle of mine sat through the whole film of Henry V. *She hardly moved, she was absolutely entranced. And afterwards, she asked such interesting things. She wanted to know all about Latin, and what was history and what was made up, and we had a jolly good natter about Shakespeare, who she knew about already from when I took her to London that time . . .*

She probably added that Kenneth Branagh was *dishy*. She always was saucy like that.

You remember that conversation. It was the ladder out the hole. Eating lunch at her dark wood table, butter dripping down your chin. Her great big mind decanting all she knew into you, until the universe sewed up its rip.

She explained how the film was first a play by Shakespeare, and, before that, it was historical fact. You kept pressing her to confirm what was real. It was important to know this, to put the straight lines back.

But no. Things only got trickier.

There's no such thing, she said, really, as Truth.

That Shakespeare took the facts and made them *feel* true. And then the film did the same. And in fact, probably, the people who recorded the battle in the first place put their own *interpretation* – a new word, she wrote it down for you – on it too.

She found her big book of Shakespeare. The words were tiny, the pages thin. She licked her finger to leaf through them – an action you'd soon start copying – until she landed on *Henry V*.

See – she pointed – He tells us right at the beginning that he's going to make it up a bit: *Oh, for a muse of fire that would ascend the brightest heaven of invention.*

She performed it theatrically in a deep posh voice.

And that actually we have to help him make it up. It's *our* imaginations that bring it to life.

She found another line for evidence:

Our *imaginary forces* — see?

Your faces were so close, squinting together at the pages, that you saw how huge her eyes looked, magnified through her specs.

She continued translating the text for you:

> *Your thoughts* — imaginations — *must deck our kings* — that means dress them — *carry them here, there, jumping o'er times* — so it's 1400s but it feels like now — *turning the accomplishment of many years* — because it's not just the battle, it's the before and afterwards — *into an hourglass* — that's another word for sand timer . . .

You could have said — Yes! I know that feeling! That sand timer! — but you didn't know how.

It wasn't words for you yet. Just a feeling you couldn't identify, a strange one you weren't sure you wanted to feel again.

It took until now to isolate that moment. To acknowledge and articulate it, to make it make sense. To let it take its place in your becoming. To name it: an awakening. An emergence of self.

The moment you first understood what words do.

When you first felt Time expand beyond clocks.

Experienced becoming others, and your own becoming through those others.

That your one little body housed thousands of selves.

This was the catalyst. You began writing and writing. Poetry, stories, plays. You and your gran wrote a novel together. You have it still, bound on your shelf.

Thirty years later, you're still chasing that feeling – of something so powerful, so transformative you dissolve. But the intensity won't come again. You worked too hard to make your world solid, and now you know too much, you can't shake it loose.

Perhaps that's why you hold tight to this memory, like you're saving it from a fire, or a flood. No special event. Nothing to photograph. Just beans on toast with your gran.

You were seven years old.

It was autumn.

And you'd just finished watching a film.

The Accordion of Categories

The Brother and Sister are miners. They have their very own mine. They march down the garden in the morning, carrying their plastic spades, singing heigh-ho. Past the elephant-ear bush full of ladybirds. Under the big sheets, blowing on the line. Over the planks and into the dirt pit, where there's treasure underground. So far they've found old coins and three trilobites, which are two hundred million years old.

The Sister finds a rock with glinty bits.

Diamonds! she says, showing the Brother.

She knows it isn't diamonds, but it's fun to pretend. The Brother is two, and knows nothing. She is five, and knows everything in the world. At least, everyone says she does. And maybe she did once. But now she's not so sure.

There used to be categories, nice clean categories, with facts and things that went into each one. Each day of her life, especially since school started, they'd been expanding, multiplying, out and out. How delicious it was, the thrill of new categories, the buzz of more facts, going on and on. Like the universe was made of boxes locked in boxes locked in boxes, and she was getting a big jangly bunch of keys at last.

But recently, the categories have been getting wiggly and complicated. Things jump out their boxes. Even people. Even her.

Adults aren't allowed in their mine. They can't see the Adults so think the Adults can't see them. They don't know their mother is watching from the window as she scrubs the morning porridge off their bowls. They don't know that Toby-Dog, sleeping under the washing line, has one droopy eye open, watching over his wards.

Their father is somewhere or anywhere. Their gran is at the castle, at work. Their auntie's doing a shift at the crisp factory. They hope she'll bring a box of duds home.

The Sister puts the rock in their treasure chest. The Brother gets it out again and puts it in his mouth.

The Brother and Sister live in a town that was nothing till the steelworks arrived. Then houses, shops, schools, churches, factories, playgrounds rose from the clod, and twelve thousand men, like their grandad, came down from Scotland, promised houses and jobs.

So the Brother and Sister live in England that's also Scotland. Rangers and Celtic. Highland Games. Irn-Bru. Their dad's side, Glaswegian. Their mum's side, English. A hard side. A soft side. One for steel. One for books.

Of course there are many sides, and no sides, but the world comes to children through opposites and pairs. Yes/no. Boy/girl. Good/bad.

As if the only way to know what you are, is to know first what you are not.

Maybe that's why the Brother points at everything, but never at himself.

Their mining isn't going well today. It's hot and the ground is dry. Their dad had said if they keep digging they'll reach Australia. It's been a long time and they're still not there. The Sister wants the trowel, but its category is Sharp Things. If her dad was here, he'd use the metal spade.

The Sister doesn't like the sun, but her dad does. His skin is always very, very brown. Maybe if he comes home again, he'll blow up the paddling pool and they'll laugh and splash around. When it's hot, he takes his top off, and she can see all the pictures on his skin. Not like normal pictures. His are there forever. He lets her try to pinch, pull, peel them off. It never hurts him. Nothing does.

All the men have these pictures. It's a category women and children aren't in.

The Sister is glad she doesn't have to have them. She went with her dad once and saw how it's done. The room smelt funny and the music was loud. He lay down, on a bed like the dentists, and his friend with gold teeth started up a kind of drill. Only it wasn't a drill, it was a *needle* and it went *inside his skin*. He pretended it tickled, but she didn't believe him. Needles are the worst thing in the whole entire world.

Thinking about needles makes her shivery, so she sits on the edge of Australia and watches ants instead. Ants always move in a line. Maybe there's a line of them – an army, they're called – that starts here and goes through the centre of the Earth. Maybe there's a girl just like her, in Australia, watching the other end of the line. Maybe the girl's dad is there, a nice dad, with a proper spade, helping her dig to England. Maybe he cuddles her and brings her ice cream. Maybe they'll dig so hard they'll pop up here, in her mine.

Thinking about this makes the Sister feel funny. She stamps on the ants with her boot.
The Brother stamps too. She tells him to stop it.

She orders the Brother to start digging. Australia is 9,000 miles away. It is going to take a very long time.

Actually, it is 9,442 miles away. The Sister likes numbers. They're right or wrong.

She knows her gran's phone number and her dad's car number plate by heart, and everyone's birthdays, which she writes in a book, and how many centimetres she is and how much the Brother weighs, and all her times tables already up to ten.

When she looks at things, numbers appear on them, like the metal number 30 on their door, but in her mind. Like if she looks at their mine, she sees 19, 6 and 38, because it's nineteen steps long and six steps wide, and thirty-eight marches from the open back door.

The Brother and Sister live in a town made of numbers. Record statistics for unemployment, illiteracy, addiction, domestic violence, spousal murder, infant death, crime. Before they were born, Margaret Thatcher closed the steelworks; now her name is like a swear word and the Adults boo when she comes on TV.

The Sister doesn't know these numbers. If she did, she would see them looming all over her street, her home. The people she loved would become walking numbers, and if she looked in the mirror, she would be one too.

She doesn't know that these numbers are all her mother thinks about as she watches her children grow.

She is working on a plan. They could still get out. There is time.

The Sister doesn't know these numbers, but she knows them as feelings at the blurry edges of her world. She knows there are categories for Safe Places and Not Safe Places, and Good People and Bad People, who do Good Things and Bad Things.

When she was little like the Brother they were obvious.

> Not Safe: hot things, sharp things, high things, strangers, dog poo, chewing gum, roads.

> Not Good: lying, stealing, Thatcher, swearing, weapons even when they're pretend, sugary things except on Fridays, going downstairs after bedtime, Digging For Gold (which means picking your nose).

But there are Bad People and Bad Things and Bad Places that nobody tells you about. You just sense it in your bones. And then it gets complicated, because it's not like maths or pointing, you can't ask anyone if you're right or wrong. Not the teachers, not your family, not any adults, because sometimes they pretend things are fine when they're not.

Like injections. But also like other things.

Things you musn't ask about, and also musn't tell.

The Sister knows when something is Not Okay, because she gets the same feeling as being in a car.

She gets more travel sick than anyone thought a child could be. Even just five minutes down the road. Nobody sits next to her on school trips, so she always has the special seat by the teacher at the front. This is not the way the Sister likes to feel special. The best way to make adults happy is not to worry them. Why doesn't her stomach know?

The Brother never gets travel sick, and it's humiliating, how the adults use his bum-wipes to mop her mouth, then bin them in one of his nappy sacks – that are meant to smell nice but make her gag, like the perfume she made for her mum in the garden by leaving daisies in water to rot.

Her gran had got her Sea-Bands – elastic bracelets, with plastic knobbly bits that go on your pulse, which is your heartbeat in your wrists. They came in their own little box with a ship on it and she wishes she could wear them all the time. Because you can feel travel sick even when you're not travelling.

You can feel travel sick when things are just wrong.

Like when she couldn't figure out how to spell the -*ing* sound. The heat in her belly, this twisting inside, the way her heart moved up her chest like she'd swallowed it, everything blurry spinny hot fast slow.

Like when her teacher sent her alone to find a pigeonhole and she didn't know what it was, looked in the playground, in the trees, running frantic down corridors, though the rule said Don't Run.

Like when she was drawing at the kitchen table. Her mum and auntie always have Radio Four on, and if she listens when they don't think she's listening, she can impress them by saying grown-up things. The news was all about Ethiopia. It said twenty-four children starve to death every day. She calculated that was one an hour, and announced it proudly, but the Adults just looked sad.

When Bad Things happened, she could feel all the categories squeezing scrunching squishing into each other, like that film they'd watched at school about wearing your seatbelt, when a car crashed into a wall and all the metal crumpled up, even the dolls inside pretending to be people, this big solid thing becoming flatter than a plate.

The Sister got the idea of categories from her animal encyclopedia, which is her favourite and most precious book. It's huge and heavy, she got it from her uncle, you have to carry it in both hands. It's meant for grown-ups not children, so it doesn't stop at Mammals and Reptiles, like school. There are Kingdoms and Classes and Species and Orders and Phylums and Genuses and more, and although it is complicated, the book makes it easy with a diagram like a family tree.

She knows about family trees because her gran is making one. There's your *immediate* family, her gran had explained, like the people in your home, and then branches and branches going back through history, connecting you to everyone, even people you've never met.

Probably all the way back to monkeys, then lizards, then dinosaurs, and the Big Bang before that. Her gran explained the Big

Bang with a fruit bowl. Life emerged from everything splintering, tumbling, out, out, out.

The Brother wheels his dumper truck over the mine. He loads it with soil then tips the soil down the hole. The more he pours into it, the more she has to dig out again, leaning over on her knees and clawing at the hole.

Stop! You're ruining it! We'll never get to Australia!

Suddenly, the ground gives way beneath her, an earthquake, a landslide, beneath her knees, and she's in the hole and the earth's slipping onto her, and her body's going travel sick, erupty spinny red.

The Brother doesn't stop. So she clambers out and pushes him. She throws his truck and pinches his arm. She grabs hold and doesn't let go of him, like he has pictures on his skin that she's trying to squeeze out.

She likes hurting him. It makes her feel better. Her heart returns to its heart-place. Guts return to her guts.

The Sister lets go. The Brother starts crying. Toby-Dog slinks over and nuzzles her face.

Now she feels better, she suddenly feels terrible. Like the person who did the hurting wasn't her, but someone else.

What was that person? A Bad Person Who Hurts People. She jumps out of her category and in with the Men. But that's not right either. What is her category? She wants to be with her mum, her auntie, her gran.

Their mother is walking towards them, the white sheets behind her billowing on the line, the tall white daisies bowing as she passes. Her mother is beautiful. She never jumps out of her category. She is always the same. Always Good.

Hello darlings, her mother says gently, scooping the Brother up into her arms.

She never gets angry. Never raises her voice. She often says Sorry, even when she hasn't done anything. Good people say sorry all the time.

I made him sad, the Sister says. I'm sorry.

The Sister leans forward and gives the Brother a kiss.

Categories used to be simple for People. But more and more often now, they're not.

Scottish-Gran – her dad's mum – was a problem. Once a month, their dad would pick them up and go to the Scottish grandparents' house. It stank of stew and ashtrays. Everything was black and brown and grey, and you weren't supposed to touch anything, and time went very slow there. They had thick Glaswegian accents, like their home still lived in their throat.

They had a noisy big dog with a choker chain that slammed itself repeatedly against the hallway door. The children had to be brave if they needed the bathroom because it meant creeping past him at the bottom of the stairs.

There were three good things in the house. One was the biscuit tin full of caramel wafers, another was the beautiful dead butterflies on the wall, and the third was their grandad, their one chance of escape.

He would sit in the kitchen, with the door ajar into the living room, where the Brother and Sister sat while their dad and Scottish-Gran fought. Scottish-Gran was always angry, which scared the Sister, but also fascinated her, like all things she couldn't work out. What category was this person? Men did anger. Women did love.

Scottish-Gran always sat in her armchair. They never saw her move. The ashtray piling up next to her. The smell of Opium perfume. Dark hair and dark eyes, that the Sister had inherited, although she wanted to be fairer like her mum, brother, auntie and gran.

At some point in these visits, their grandad would put his coat on and take them to the mobile grocers that drove around the estate. He'd buy them sweets and a comic. Then they'd come back and it would be time to go.

They always left in the middle of an argument. Their grandad never got involved. So they liked him best, and they knew people respected him, he had been a foreman at the works, and played football really well.

42

But they also sensed that the Adults didn't like him. Their dad said once he used to *give him the belt*. Whatever that meant, it apparently wasn't a good thing. The Sister kept an eye on their grandad's belt but he never gave it to her.

Last Sunday, Scottish-Gran asked the Sister what she was reading. It was Roald Dahl's *Revolting Rhymes*. Scottish-Gran asked her to read one. The Sister wanted to make her happy, so she did.

Scottish-Gran only bought them Jesus books so the Sister chose a poem set in a church. It was funny, because it rhymed *knickers* with *vicar's* which she thought would make Scottish-Gran laugh. Everybody liked Roald Dahl. It was one category everyone was in.

But Scottish-Gran didn't laugh. It made the arguing much worse.

The Sister was mortified. Crumpled like the car did. Squished crashed crushing like the dummies in the car.

Sometimes, at bedtime, her head is so full of things, full of all the things that have happened in the day, and so many words and facts and stories, and bad things like a video playing over and over again, and all of it getting noisier and bigger and over-lapping, and her head gets very loud, and she can't make it stop.

When she gets like that at bedtime – like she needs to turn inside out, like when the hoover starts roaring so her mum knows to empty it – when she gets all sick hot dizzy volcanoey – she lies extremely still, holds her breath and does times tables.

Then she lines all her teddies across her and counts them in order again and again. She pulls the covers over them, so they have equal amounts of blanket, so they know they are equally loved.

Loved/unloved. Asleep/awake. She doesn't know the words yet for all the feelings in between.

She thinks about Mrs Jukes's accordion. How you have to pull it out, until it won't go out any more, then you have to squeeze it back in. The music only comes if you do that repeatedly, out then in again, out then in.

Why did no one warn her life was like that? Out then in again, out then in.

Why did no one warn her the categories don't go on expanding. Not bigger and neater, but messier and small. A fact, thing or person that belonged in one box could suddenly belong elsewhere – or nowhere at all.

This is why she's been feeling funny lately. Her mind always unpacking then repacking every box. The pile getting bigger of all the stuff that doesn't belong anywhere. Sometimes she is in that pile. Even her.

She thinks about the seatbelt video. If she's not careful, she'll be squashed.

Her maths book asks: *How many people are in your family?*

Four.

She wants to write 'six', to include her gran and auntie. Or maybe seven, with Toby-Dog.

Or maybe the real answer should be all of them plus her teddies, which is seven plus twenty-three, which is thirty, which is the number house she lives at, which comes as a shock, as coincidences do, so that thirty will always seem to her a magic number, like God reached through the clouds and drew it on her palm.

Or maybe she should count the names on the family tree her gran made, which would be hundreds, all connected to her.

She asks the teacher if it means *immediate family*. The teacher says Yes and is very impressed. So the Sister rubs out 'Four' and writes 'Three'.

Which is funny, because three is less than four. But when it's the three of them – her, her mum, her brother – the feeling she gets is enormous, like you couldn't even count it on your hands.

But they do try and count it. They count it at bedtime, when their mum and auntie tuck them up in bed. They don't use categories and labels and numbers. Even the Adults can't count love.

How much do I love you? their mum says, kissing them.

45

As much as . . .

A pause, they all giggle, trying to think of silly things.

> As much as . . . the Sister says . . . every dromedary camel in the Sahara, dancing on tightropes from here to Jupiter, balancing every book ever written on their heads!

> Asmuzas . . . powidge! tries the Brother, understanding it, giggling, amazed at himself for slotting another jigsaw piece into the world.

Her auntie is always the funniest –

> As much as . . . a twenty-armed octopus flipping pancakes so high that they sizzle on the sun and bounce back into our tummies!

And always, their mother gives the finisher – the phrase they're waiting for, that confirms all this, and more, is true –

> . . . all the way to the moon and back, with a cherry on top.

They never did dig to Australia. But their mother did dig deep enough to get them away. They would live by the sea in Cornwall. They would not become numbers. Not the wrong kind at least.

Breaking the Chain

Hope was three hundred miles away. They'd only been married a month. One-way coach tickets, instead of wedding presents.

Fresh start for the both of yous, her ma had said.

This wasn't what the young wife had dreamed of. But her ma warned:

Stay here an' yer bairns'll rot.

Twelve thousand men responded to the advert, getting off their jacksies to hoach their way out the pish. Never mind it was England. It was houses and jobs. If the newlyweds had stayed, they'd have lived in her ma's bedroom. Her ma on the sofa, Wee Eddie in the hall. It would have been okay. It's not the size of your home, but who's in it. But that was the problem, when the men had no jobs.

The house in the new town was too big for them. Only enough stuff for one room. Nothing to tidy. It smelt of paint. Only one ashtray, on a doilly on the table. There should be one spilling on the arm of every chair.

How many rooms, her ma asked.

Four, Ma.

But it was eight rooms. *Eight*. An upstairs *and* downstairs.

Eight rooms, empty and silent. Husband at work. No one choking up the place. She couldn't get used to it. Felt somehow ashamed. The slum still inside her was strong.

She heard a man shout in the background of the phone line, his fist banging on the glass.

Y'alright there, Ma? I don't like you using that phonebox.

Get on, you've just got soft.

I'll get you a landline.

What do I want that for? Everyone'll be knocking on mah door! Anyway, what about that Jeanette who went down w' yous? Or Margaret, she's a nice gal . . .

Margaret and Jeanette had been over. Mainly to compare their houses with hers. But it hadn't been like the old days. They'd nibbled their shortbread, not dropping a crumb. This shared mistrust of such niceness. They didn't joke rude and bicker like they should. Nobody swore. Like living in church.

Soon enough, youse'll have kiddies and you won't get a minute.

Will you be movin' in then? When there's bairns. Like we said?

We'll have to see. There's Wee Eddie.

He's twenty!

But unemployment made men stay boys. If they had wives, then the wives became their mothers. If they had mothers, then their mothers became wives.

The husbands down here though were real men. For the first time, they all had jobs. They worked hard and the wives admired them. They breathed them in, when they came home full of sweat. When they kissed them, they tasted of burning, because the steelworks got into their throats. They'd be ordered straight up to the bathroom, warned not to touch anything till they'd scrubbed off the soot.

And the wives didn't mind, when the men went drinking. They'd earned it. Deserved a break. Still the wisest took a tenner out the wage slip when their husbands were putting on a fresh shirt.

The wife hoped and prayed for a daughter. Didn't want the responsibility of raising a son. A daughter came first. She was lucky. But then came identical twin boys.

They're a handful! her ma said, when she visited.

Her ma never did move in.

The wife didn't like them being born English, but the town came with everything to raise them Scots. She fed Glasgow to them, like she was stuffing them with home, stew and broth and Mr Brain's Meat Faggots, or as the kids called them, Mr Faggot's Brains, and Irn-Bru downed so they could stack the cans as targets.

The relief when the kids spoke Weegie. Everyone in the town kept their tongue. They recreated Glasgow, to pretend they'd never left it. Kept up the traditions, the football, the churches, kept up the dances, the Highland Games. Kept up the rivalries that once brought battles, but here, even brawling brought the belonging they craved.

The town might be new, but they didn't have to be new with it. When they realised that, they sank back and dropped crumbs. The houses became homes filled with ornaments and toys, and trophies on the mantlepiece from football or darts. Burn marks round the ashtrays on the armchairs. Bright dead butterflies in frames on the walls.

It was warmer down here. The streets were safer. Even in winter, the kids played outside. All that steel built smart new play-grounds. No glass or pish on the streets. No jobbies or glue-bags or needles. No one would steal their bikes. Never mind she had to check which way the wind blew. The wrong direction and they'd come back choking on soot.

There were fireworks, not just in November. Explosions in the sky when there were accidents at the works. Accidents came almost daily. It increased their pride, this dangerous work. When one of the lads wasn't careful on the crane gears, he'd jolt the giant ladle, molten steel spilling out. Sparks would shoot up, all the kids running, oohing and aahing, saying *My da did that! No, it were my da, you fibber! No it were my da, I promise yous! On yer bike!*

Twice a year they'd make a trip back to Glasgow. Turn up in their car, prezzies in the boot. Buy every round. Take them all out for dinner. Some said they'd gone posh. Most didn't. After all, the wives always sent money home.

She used to call her ma every day. As the years passed, it became once a week. Her ma agreed to the landline because she couldn't keep hobbling down the tenement stairwells with her leg, especially not in winter when it was baltic, and especially not now there were so many jakeys on the streets.

Hoo's the bairns?

Doin' fine Ma.

An' Ted?

He's fine.

Treatin' yer right?

Aye, fine.

51

And you hen?

I'm fine too, Ma.

Good, that's good.

What else to say? What other lie?

The wife rings off, lights a Benson & Hedges, turns up the telly so next door won't hear her cry.

What to say?

> You were wrong, Ma. No new future here. A new life maybe, but not the right life.

To say —

> Ma, they're closing down the steelworks. I know you heard about it, and I told you Ted's job's fine. But it's not. He's laid off like all of them. Every man in the town, Ma. It's no better than Easterhouse now.

It's the same — a town of angry bored men, making mothers out their wives. Just the same — the husbands sitting round all day, smoking, as the wives lift their feet to hoover under them, as they change the ashtrays, make the dinners with no thanks.

Just the same — the dinners back to offal cuts, unless you got lucky in the meat raffle at the club, which is the only place here still open, because like back home, there's money for nothing but the drink.

Just the same violence and brawling. Every wife dreading the score on a Rangers v Celtic night. Caking their faces with make-up to hide what happened after a bad result.

Stay here an' yer bairns w' rot, you said? Well, Ma – my children are rotting alright. I tell you they're fine but they're not. They're worse than we kids ever were. We were wild, aye, but we had you family. We had all of yous to keep us in line.

The boys, Ma? Aye, they're grand. They play football which I know makes yous proud. But you know what else, Ma? They're wee scampin' bastards, and I don't know what to do. Skippin' school, drinkin', gi'in people a doin'. Coming home with their bruises, Ted addin' a fair few more. Ted's belt's aff more than an these days.

I had the polis here, Ma. The polis.

New life? Aye right. You can stuff it up yer arse.

She prayed the boys would grow out of their antics. Find nice lassies. Have children. Settle down. And she must have prayed right, because they did. A little earlier than she'd have liked, for one. Went with his lassie from fourteen. Sixteen and they assembled for the wedding photo, Weegies one side, English lot the other.

The photographer had moved her next to the other mother-in-law. *More balanced*, he'd said, *You look so alike*. No, she'd thought,

We're bare opposites. Her cloud of white hair. Mine coal-black. Her husband had nae been a works man. Insurance. Thought they were posh.

Her daughter-in-law's family were soft. No trouble, though she'd rather the other in-laws weren't divorced. Divorce can run in families, she'd seen that. Mothers put the idea in daughters' heads.

She could only pray her boy would be a good husband and they'd have good children, and they would never ever leave.

How much you take with you, when you go. Things you can't get rid of. Things you can't get back.

★ ★ ★ ★

Hope is three hundred miles away. The daughter-in-law decides it's time to leave the steel-town now. Her children are four and six. She needs a different life for them all.

The daughter-in-law has been taking an evening class. Psychology – why we are how we are. Suddenly everything makes sense to her: brains and behaviour. How it all starts in childhood. In what we see. What we learn.

It's funny, but lots of theories come from twin studies. Every time the teacher mentions one, the other women look at her. Her husband is an identical twin. If she makes him a case study, he'll shrink in her mind. The fascination of it makes her stronger. He has force, but she'll have knowledge. She'll grow beyond this. And he'll never grow.

Her children will grow beyond this: her single mission in life. She is learning how things come in patterns. The looping of ancestry. What we carry in our bones. How the children end up like the parents, and the parents like their parents, right back to the start.

She won't have that for her children. She must be the last link in the chain.

She sees them all, all the town, wrapped in chains now. The locked links jangling on and on. The violence, addiction and poverty. The anger, abuse and dirt. The ignorance. The stuckness. The protests. And the men, and the men, and the men.

Stand up. Speak up. Be bold. Wrap your children in more love than they can know. Hold your own. Question everything.

No force in the world will take this knowledge from her now.

★ ★ ★ ★

Hoo's the family, hen?

Aye fine, Ma.

Those wee grandchildren?

Aye, grand.

Thanks for the piccies. You must be so proud of them.

[Silence]

That Holly's got the same look as you and her da. Those chocolate button eyes.

[Silence]

You there, hen?

I've got to go, Ma. Love to Eddie. I'll give yous a bell.

What else to say? She shakes, lights a cigarette. Gulps brandy from her glass.

How do you tell your mother you know now what she went through. How sorry you are that you left.

That three hundred miles is a bloody long way away.

How will she keep an eye on them, now they've gone.

She would cry, but it has long dried out of her. She knows other women who would laugh.

They unnerve her, these women, at the bingo. Lose all their money and just laugh. Husbands die, they cry, then start laughing. There was one woman, Anne. Not a Scot. I've got cancer, Anne had said. And she'd laughed. At the funeral, people remembered how fun she was. How lightly she took life, even through blows. Never lost that warm sense of humour, they said, as if that was a mark of a good person somehow.

What was so wrong with feeling angry? Oh she's angry. Oh she could shout.

She remembers the women huddled cackling back in Glasgow. Joshing and gossiping, choking on laughs. All of them, living in that tenement – all those bodies, the noise, stink and rows – and not a good hand to deal between them. But no. They'd laugh and laugh.

If she'd have stayed, would she now be laughing?

> My daughter-in-law's leaving with my grandkids, and
> my son's a right bastard, heehaw!

* * * *

The daughter-in-law has two brothers and a sister, all of them close and kind and good. Her sister had lived with them, another mother to the children, and her brothers, against the odds, are gentle and soft. How could she leave them. Take the children away from them. Three hundred miles is far.

> It's the right thing to do, they reassure her. Fresh
> start. It'll be better for you all.

They move into a wreck of a terrace, at the top of a hill above the sea. Never mind it's been squatted in for years. Never mind it's a carcass – no electrics, pipes or floorboards, every last morsel stolen or sold.

She feels the house has chosen them somehow. They will fix each other, with strength, patience, and hope.

She teaches herself electrics and plumbing. Works cleaning jobs and kitchen jobs while the children are at school, saving for tools or timber or wiring. She asks lots of questions at the hardware shop. She paints the front door bright yellow. There is nothing she can't do with a saw.

Sometimes, when the children bring new friends home, their parents pick them up and say *This was our squat!* She lets them inside, as they shake their heads laughing, with shame or nostalgia or both, and they find their names on the walls where the graffiti hasn't been scrubbed off yet.

They live in a story-house. Now they'll make their own stories.

Her sister comes with paint in bright colours. One room becomes citrus orange and yellow, one deep pink like a womb. They get glass paint for the windows, and fill the panel in the front door with gold.

Summer comes, and she's planting, calling her mum for advice on what would grow where. The passionflower loves the climate and grows prolifically all over the yard. By the front door, a window-box of pansies, that she and her sister call Mrs Evans, but she can't remember why.

Everything is possible: her mantra. Her children never know they are poor. She turns poverty into an adventure, fun and creative. It's a game, to wait for the co-op to put red stickers on bargains. It's exciting to pick your Christmas presents from the catalogue in July. Walking for miles is better than having a car, because you can talk, and play games, and notice things, and skip, and stop to find snails and usher beetles off paths.

They make everything they need. If they can't make it, they borrow it. Hire tools from the tool shop, books from the library, trade toys at the swap shop, go to the Scrap Store for arts and crafts. They scrunch elastic bands around stained bedsheets and bathe them in bright water to dye and look new.

The mother still studies psychology. A degree now, with the Open University, part time, in between cleaning jobs, the children and the house. Those things are all present tense. Her studies, the future.

Any time she doubts the move, she remembers her children's brains. Holds on to the fact that those young brains have plasticity. She is laying down new wiring, and not just in the house.

★ ★ ★ ★

If hope isn't three hundred miles away, maybe it's further.

I've booked a wee trip, Ma. To Spain.

Aye, nice, hen. Yer takin the grandkids?

No, Ma. Just mahsel.

Yous should all come here soon.

They're busy with school.

They're clever you said?

Aye Ma. Right clever. They see school like we see church.

Her daughter-in-law writes to her sometimes. Sends photos and tells her about the kids. For a while, her son went to and fro.

59

Said he'd do anything, he'd change. They'd get back together then he'd mess up again. She'd give him a tongue-lashing every time.

An' yer pals? You mustn't get lonely.

I'm no lonely, Ma.

Going on holiday on your own!

Last year, she'd won at the bingo and her friend said, Why not get away. She'd been away twice since then. Spain next week. She likes the flamenco and the sun. People speak to her in Spanish because she looks like them. In the winter, she'll see her other son in the Canaries. He's made good for himself. A teacher. Spanish wife. How could two sons, identical, be so different. What had she done.

How's yer knitting coming on?

Doin' bears now. Wee bears to sell at church.

For charity?

Aye. Best be gettin' on. Got twenty of the wee buggers to do.

She picks up the needles. She's always liked knitting. Likes following patterns, till her fingers learn them in her bones. Looping and tightening and circling. So simple, so predictable, these repetitions. Why wasn't life like that.

She wonders how many jumpers and cardigans she's knitted for the grandkids over the years. Her daughter-in-law always admired them. She can picture her granddaughter Holly wearing a peach cardigan, reading on the floor.

Read me a poem, she'd asked Holly.

Anything to stop the shouting from her son.

Holly thought a moment, flicking the pages. Then she stood and recited the poem as if on stage.

At the end, Holly laughed. She was meant to laugh with her. They were meant to share something in that laugh. But she didn't laugh. She was fuming. Holly's face fell apart.

She was expecting to hear a poem about – what? Flowers, or the creatures on God's earth. Love and sweetness and goodness. But what she read was filth about a middle-aged virgin, groped by the vicar at a church bazaar.

Her son had laughed. Not at the poem. At her. At her face, and Holly's face. He'd laughed and laughed.

What happened next? Maybe Ted took them for comics. She can't remember anything except how that line went round her head –

I made a grab. I caught the mouse,/now right inside my knickers

– that final line hanging in the air, her grandchild's voice so innocently saying it –

A mouse my foot! It was a HAND!/Great Scott! It was the vicar's!

Awful. Just awful. Disgusting.

And yet now – a tickling rises up in her throat.

A fizzing, bubbling up from the depths of her.

Knickers. Vicar's.

Her mouth twitches. She laughs. It was funny! Appalling – but funny! And how funny that she'd thought it so bad!

She's laughing, crossing her legs so she doesn't wet herself. Laughing so much the dog comes and barks.

Then she's crying, because they've gone, and they never laughed together.

The dog's still barking. So she gives him a smack.

★ ★ ★ ★

The daughter-in-law gets her degree in psychology. It takes ten years, off and on. The future is now the present. Her daughter's eighteen and about to leave. To South Africa, the other side of the world. The daughter who once said to her, *If I stay here, I'll rot.*

She hides the pain the distance brings her. She'd raised her children to have the whole world. To feel freedom. Be anyone. Go anywhere. Question everything. Grab experiences. Be bold.

Still, she's grateful her son is still home with her. Grateful he's soft and gentle, like his uncles, against the odds.

They still live in the house on the hilltop, with its bright walls painted and repainted every hue. Now she wants white, clean spaces. Her heart and her children's hearts are filled with colour. She'd banished the greyness. That one job was done.

Sometimes she thinks of her former in-laws. Just the mother-in-law now, cancer got Ted. Their house, grey and brown. All those ornaments. Dead butterflies on the wall.

She wonders what comes first – sad houses or sad people.

Her daughter woke up once and said she'd had a funny dream. Scottish-Gran was dancing naked and setting fire to the house.

★ ★ ★ ★

Hi, Ma.

It's no Ma, it's Eddie.

What you bellin' me for?

Ma's gone.

Deed?

Nah! Aff to Mallorca. Left mah tea with a note. Says she got yer postcard an' she thought, Och sod it. Gave Uncle Terry al the dough oot her jar. He sorted her a ticket.

When's she back?

She dunnae say. I'm fumin'. Who's gonnae iron mah
shirts?

What to say? She's laughing. She's laughing, a foreign sound to
these walls.

Quit bellying, this is serious!

I'm sorry!

But she's not sorry and the laughing won't stop.

Who's gonnae—

Och Eddie, do it yersel man. Yer no mammy's wee
boy, get on!

Imagine her saying that! Brazen! But how good it felt! What else
might she say!

She lights a cigarette but can't smoke for laughing. Stub it out!
Why smoke! Why sit here all day! Why knit these teddy bears!
Why have the telly blathering on!

She jumps off her chair and rips the wires out the TV. Rips the
cord out the phone. Hurls her tea at the wall.

Will she knit? No! Flicks open her lighter, and drops it into the
knitting basket full of charity bears. How quickly it catches!
What else? She must feed it. Ted's coat. Why hang on to it?
Family photographs. Burn! Burn!

Open the dresser and get the crate of duty-free cigarettes. Tip them all out onto the flames. Bye-bye handbags, tea cosies, hairnets, antimacassars, Spanish lace. Bye-bye Bible. Ta-ta God. What did you ever do for me, with my knees prayed raw.

Perfume next. What was the point of it? Perfume! How ridiculous, covering up how we smell! Watch the explosions like the fireworks from the steelworks. Licking the ceiling, flaring the rug.

What next? Her wedding dress. Her wedding ring. Sod it – all her clothes.

She pushes her armchair into the flames, feeling new strength in her, like she's young, cackling as it catches, the smell of burning leather like the smell of the abattoir down the road.

She's cackling, ripping her clothes off, she's naked and cackling and starting to dance.

The butterflies! She must free the butterflies! Fifty years they've been waiting to fly! She smashes their glass cages and they fly to her, land on her nakedness, join her dancing round the flames.

She opens all the windows and watches them flit past her, and she's laughing and crying and waving them goodbye. The neighbours are screaming at her through the windows. She gives them the finger, breasts jaggling. She tears the curtains down.

Crazy? Youse the crazy ones! I'm free!

She calls the dog and unclasps his choke-chain. He licks her and nuzzles her bare skin.

Poor boy, she says. Why did we put that on you?

It's heavy that chain. She drops it on the fire. So heavy, it makes the fire go out. She lies on the floor, watching it glowing. A circle of circles, end to end. How the glowing spreads slowly, each link passing on the heat. Hypnotic. A spell. Pink green purple. Orange gold red, then blue.

She remembers lying on the road like this as a toddler, stroking a puddle, to make the petrol colours dance.

She watches as the solid links weaken, grow darker.

Dark like a bruise.

Then bend. Then snap.

Good Toes Naughty Toes

It begins like this: good toes/naughty toes. Toddlers in tutus, skipping round the Working Men's Club, fluttering giddy fairy wings in and out the tables where men sit nursing the first of the day. Mid-morning light streams gold through the fag smoke as little satin tiptoes schlup the sticky floor. Big Pat sets up the meat raffle. Her daughter scrubs the bar.

They sit in a circle and ruffle out their tutus, stretching their legs out in front of them as they're told. *Good toes, naughty toes*, Miss Dee-Anne sings, as they flex their clumsy feet up and down.

The Dancer is three years old. The piano is the most beautiful sound she has ever heard. She screws her little eyes shut and concentrates. The Dancer has good toes, from her very first class.

The good toes go with her, when they leave the steel town for Cornwall, and get her noticed by Miss Anya. All dance teachers are Misses, because to dance is to be pure, beyond the darkness of the world.

67

The Dancer knows the darkness all too well. But when she dances, it disappears. Everything that is heavy in life leaves her, as soon as the music plays. The world is light, and she is light inside it. No effort to leap across the studio, to stand on her toes. She sails through each grade examination. Her good toes get her noticed, though that's not why she dances at all.

The Dancer is made of an otherness. Not body. Not mind. Something else. Something more.

This is why everyone watches her. The story of elsewhere she tells with her bones.

The Dancer is eleven, on a train with her mother, rattling over the River Tamar suspension bridge, behind them Cornwall, ahead of them the world.

The Dancer has her nose in a book as usual, but secretly she is trying to read her mother's mind. She has long suspected her mother can read hers. That's why she never swears or thinks anything bad. Recently she's been trying to develop telepathy. She has come to see people as radios – turn the dial slowly, listen very close, and you can start to hear things that exist between sounds.

Her mother is re-reading the audition information. She is thinking her daughter is too young and too small to let go.

The Dancer secretly concentrates. Beyond the static, she can hear her mother's bones.

I don't want to go, her mind tells her mother's mind. *I don't want to leave you. I will never leave you on your own.*

She won't leave her little brother either. Three lines alone are vulnerable. Put them together, and their triangle keeps them safe.

Once, two pitbulls attacked them. It was winter. They were on the beach. *Come to me*, the mother said to the children. They were crying and screaming. She pulled them so close. *Stand really still*, she said, *like we're one big person, and the dogs will go away.*

The Dancer and her mother get off at Paddington and hold hands through the clamour and throng, which eases with each tube stop away from the centre until they reach Richmond. Not normal London. Trees! The first time she's seen deer up close.

They set up camp in a B&B room. There's a telly just for them. In the distance, over the park, they see what they're there for: White Lodge mansion, that legendary shrine, which, if she passes the week of auditions, the Dancer will have to learn to call home.

She hadn't expected the invitation to audition. What an opportunity. Every dancer's dream. Things like this didn't happen to girls like her. The excited pride of her teacher. *The Royal Ballet!* Of course she'd go.

Her mother never said, But I would miss you.

The Dancer never said, I would miss you so much I'd rather die.

Next morning, with her ballet bun and dance bag, they walk across the deer park to White Lodge. Margot Fonteyn, Ninette de Valois, Darcey Bussell – the deer saw them all, caught the scent of their hairspray, laughed at how humans had to learn how to leap. Raised their young and battled with antlers to the sound of the piano drifting over the trees.

The foyer is tense with skinny girls and stage mums fussing over their daughters and sussing other girls out. Chandeliers, paintings, sunlight. Numbers printed on paper, given to each girl. The Dancer stays close to her mother, then looks back at her as they're herded down the hall.

She changes into her simple tights and leotard, with name labels her mother has sewn on by hand. The other girls look like proper dancers – various layers to their outfits she doesn't have, sweatpants and chiffon and crossover cardigans, the kind she's gazed at in the dance shop in Plymouth on the annual pilgrimage to buy new shoes.

There's a handmade card from her brother in her ballet bag, *Good Luck* in bubble writing next to a ballerina in pink pen. She squeezes the ear of her one-legged ballet bear, but keeps it out of sight. She has never been competitive or envious. But she feels some shame as she hangs up her stuff.

She fumbles with the safety pin to attach her number, wincing as it pricks her skin. They line up in silence in the corridor, a woman's hands on her shoulders, moving her up in the queue.

Then the studio door opens. More hands on them, moving them into rows, the woman standing back to survey them, before moving them again, like furniture in a room.

The Dancer finds herself at the front. Like always. Even though she wants to hide at the back.

She'd decided to dance as badly as possible. She had been planning how to do it on the train. Be out of time. Fake sloppy footwork. Get the wrong leg on purpose. Fall out of a turn.

But then the lid lifts on the grand piano. The music begins, and she has no choice. The ballet master paces, barking instructions. The judging panel scribbles, points and whispers, pinched pencilled eyebrows raised.

The Dancer sees herself as they must see her. Sees herself in the mirror. In the teacher's steely gaze.

She sees it all – and then she doesn't.

She is there – and then she's not.

The music plays, and she obeys it, choiceless. No plans now. There is only the dance. She closes her eyes, and finds the place she goes to. The place where nothing else exists.

She opens them again, because she's been warned by her teacher that dancers have to talk with their eyes. But she has learned how to stay in her Other Place with them open.

Sometimes it feels so magical, so profound, she could cry.

People think dancing is all about the body. But when she floats away to her Other Place, she has no weight, no bones. The world disappears there, and so does her body. It simply does what it is told.

She tamed her body to obey her, and in return it gave her pain, and then she mastered the pain, and there was nothing it could do to her any more.

In the evenings, the Dancer's mother washes her leotards in the sink, before hanging them off the bed rail to dry. Then the Dancer fills the sink with surgical spirit and holds on tight to her mother's hand.

She lifts one foot onto the rim of the sink and peels back the blisters to expose raw skin. She pulls off the toenails hanging by threads, nods once to her mother, then slides her foot in.

The pain is intense. She makes no sound. Just squeezes her mother's hand and breathes deep, until she's gasping with the burn. The foot comes out the acid. The other foot goes in. By morning, the skin will have hardened, ready to be ripped all over again.

The mother says nothing. What could she say? *Please, my child. I cannot watch you in so much pain.* But she is learning that her little girl is complicated. All she can do is try and keep her soft inside.

For the Dancer, there is no life without dancing, and there is no dancing, no life, without pain.

At the end of each class, the girls stand for scrutiny. Then numbers are called. And those numbers have to leave.

Her number isn't called on the first day. Nor the second. Nor the third. By the fourth day, she is one of a small group left. Just the medical and academic exams to go.

That evening, they go to a phonebox to tell her brother and Auntie-Mum the news. The Dancer and her mother huddle together around the receiver, two ears, two mouths, in the space for one. She wishes they could crawl through the wires away from here and snuggle up and chatter all together back home.

How amazed they all are. How excited. More than a thousand applied and she's down to the last few.

> Only twelve get in though, says the Dancer, trying to use her telepathy to reassure them it won't be her.

In the phone box, the Dancer's mother never says to her sister, *What if this really happens? How would we let her go?*

The academic exam isn't a problem. The medical is the thing she's been dreading the most.

The Dancer has a secret: she hates her body. She has hated it all her small life.

She doesn't know why or when it started. She was eight or nine when she hid in lockers to avoid the swimming pool. How disgusting and fat she thought she was. But she was locker-sized, a garden bird. PE lessons in blue gym knicks terrified her. Later, she would cover mirrors with newspaper. Sometimes she wouldn't leave the house. She hated photographs. Intimacy with the light on. Her mantra to lovers, as an adult: *Stop looking at me, you're looking, I can tell.*

Until now, dancing let her escape that.

Until now – waiting to be prodded and weighed.

Until now – lying on a trolley, a cold hand forcing down one hip. Another hand pulling her leg sideways and wrenching it above her head. Another person with a giant protractor, measuring the angles between her feet and hips, her hypermobility a prize, not a curse. Good angles/naughty angles. No Other Place now.

Her body betrays her. Gives up its secrets. The examiners murmur, nod, make notes.

What do they know about her, that she could never know? These adults, divining the adult-body inside her child-body. Predicting what kind of woman she will be.

She wants her mum to come and lift her off that bed. To say to them, *She's a child for god's sake. Leave her alone.*

But dancers are good girls. Their muteness a blessing. She stays quiet, and lets them poke.

The final day comes. Fifteen, twenty girls. Just formalities now. An interview with the director in an airy white office, looking out over the park.

The director addresses her by name. The time for numbers has passed.

> And how would you feel about being a pupil here?
> About living away from home?

The first time anyone has actually asked her. The first opportunity all week to unmute.

She knows what she is meant to say. That it would be a dream come true. An honour. All I've ever wanted. My destiny. The life I want.

The Dancer looks down. The leather chair is sticky. Her feet don't touch the floor.

> I don't want to come here, she says. I don't want to leave home. I wouldn't like it at all.

The director closes her folder. The Dancer trembles. She has done the right thing, but the right thing was wrong.

She got her wish. She didn't go to the ballet school. And when the choice came again at sixteen, she turned it down. She had a brain that kept her safer than her body. So she chose university, not the stage.

Her women saved her from the life she hadn't wanted – her mum, her auntie-mum, her gran. Not by putting her off, not by forcing her to make different choices. They gave her all the unconditional support a child could want.

But when the director had asked her that crucial question, she had answered with their voices in her own small voice.

The Dancer was more than a dancer to her women. So she became more than a dancer to herself.

She tried going back to ballet later, as an adult. Craving that Other Place. Needing to move. But despite trying to blend into the background, her Good Toes made everyone watch. She'd start at the back, but teachers brought her forward. Asked about her background. She'd oblige with a quiet CV. After White Lodge, she'd got into a different dance company, trained with famous dancers, performed in London theatres, for royalty, TV.

She doesn't tell them how they were beaten with sticks and humiliated. How one teacher had six-inch fingernails she would claw into your bum.

She doesn't tell them that after stopping dancing, she endured years of eating disorders, desperate to control her body again, bend it to her will.

She doesn't tell them about the BBC changing room, where a famous comedian let himself in and watched the girls undress.

She doesn't tell them about the only other audition she failed, and how she'd failed it because she'd never danced with a boy. She was fourteen; he older. What to do with him. How to let him touch her, take her hand.

She doesn't tell them how ballet robbed her of puberty. Hormoneless, due to the intensity of training. Amenorrhoea – no periods. Instead, her blood rite pooled out of her toes. How doctors had to force it with the Pill. The blood came so violently she'd black out. Flesh filled so suddenly her friend joked she'd had a boob job. In her leotard, she felt whaleish and sullied, her womanhood bare.

To become woman is to know blood without violence. It is also to know violence without blood.

At one of these adult classes, the teacher said, *I know you*. She even remembered the Dancer's name.

She said, I watched you dance when you were eleven.
What you had then hasn't changed.

She said, Didn't you win the—

Yes.

But the Dancer doesn't want to talk about that any more.

If life had been different, there'd have been an end to it anyway. After thirty, a dancer's body breaks. What do broken dancers think of their mothers? Who hairsprayed and scolded them in the changing rooms of their youth. Who let them go far away when they were only children. Who let them believe their worth was only located in their toes.

The Dancer is so grateful to her mother for never doing that. For never imposing on her an unlived life. She wants to hold her mother's hands now and twirl together, swaying silly circles, on a clifftop, no applause.

She's sorting through old boxes when she finds the photographs. The ones they had to send with the Royal Ballet application form. They didn't have a camera. Must have borrowed one. It would have cost her mother money to get the film printed off.

Three photos of the Dancer in a leotard. A scrawny, pale, fright-ened little bird. She remembers they'd moved the battered old sofa because the instructions said the background should be clear.

Three poses required. Good body/bad body. Good angles/naughty angles. Good toes/naughty toes.

Dancers' eyes tell stories. Luckily, the camera flash reddened hers out.

Thirty years have passed since those auditions. But in the annals of her brain, the choreography lives on. Her feet remember everything – every step, every exercise. In the kitchen, when nobody's looking, her body moves effortlessly through entire routines. No music plays, but she hears it. No teacher barks, though she hears that too.

Clap the pretty dancer. Gorge on her steps. Feast on her purity till tears wash your cheeks.

Grasp the feet of the pretty little dancer. Unbind them. Lap the blood that spills out.

Catch hold of her skirts as she spins away from you. Look into her eyes. Make her face meet the light.

Applaud her into pieces to feed you. Cheer for the beauty that lies so nobly through her pain.

Let the orchestra play. Let the orchestra play. And when the curtain falls, throw roses at her feet.

The Smell of Our Skins

1.

In 1994, we are eleven years old, and we know it's the last summer of our lives. The sun comes, rough and Cornish, and we riot just to hear the sound. Teachers struggle. Parents give up. We are ponytail hairbands coiled tight before the snap.

It is the summer we emerge, and it takes us by force. The Atlantic blows in our faces and we smell each other's skins for the very first time. Not the smells our parents lend us – fags and dogs and unwashed clothes. Not the smells that rise from our dinner plates – chip fat, bean juice, margarine. This is the sweet dank musk of our bodies, the blueprint leaked by darkening pores. We smell it on each other behind the tuckshop, in the slow dance at discos in the dark.

Beneath our uniforms, we are animals. We stink of all the things we can't yet name.

By July, we are in full bloom. We fatten and curve, or shoot up and pole out. The boys get buzzcuts and earrings, and drawl like their tongues are too big for their mouths. They pick moss out the cracks in the render and throw it at our cross-legged laps yelling PUBES. Lisa and Tamsin wear push-up bras. Jenna gets her period and four days off school. When she comes back, she is different, and we look at her like she's been gone for a very long time.

In the last few Fridays of primary school, girls go in one room, boys in another, and we're told how our insides work. Boys have lines, and girls have circles, and the lines go in the circles, and the circles let them in. We laugh, because we know it all already. Then we laugh because we know none of it at all. There's a secret that adults know about us, and no amount of diagrams can explain away the shame.

We know it's our last summer. Come September, we'll be seniors in the metal-fenced compound down the road, drinking and dry-humping, giving each other handjobs and piercings with pins. Cornwall isn't kind to childhoods, played out between caves and arcades. Before long, we'll be queuing for nightclubs, and having our tender tongues sucked dry by town men twice our age who kiss the young so they don't have to grow up. We'll say we're seventeen, they'll say they're twenty, and the lie into adulthood will be complete.

Soon, we'll be dousing ourselves in aerosols, and our own scents will be lost, before they'd even begun. But for now, we are eleven, and we smell each other, not ourselves.

We are eleven years old, and we own it, this dead-end, buzzing, rotting, stick-of-old-rock town.

2.

In 1994, we know there are many ways to die. Leukaemia, rusty nails, drowning. The brother of someone in the year below falls off the cliffs and dies. Cot death is a thing, and your shell suit could combust, and you could choke on screwballs from the ice-cream van if you swallow the gobstopper buried inside. Death by pitbull or meningitis. An airgun went off in one boy's eye. Our dentist lost his hand in a lawnmower accident and killed himself. We pass notes about it in class. How did he do it with one hand.

We are obsessed with acid rain that could burn our skins off. When it rains in the playground we huddle and shriek, like we're going to die. At Danielle's sleepover, she tells us about cancer IN YOUR BITS, and all of us fumble in the dark of our sleeping bags for lumps that couldn't be there.

We have nightmares from our history lessons. Beheadings and the plague. We do World War Two projects because we're old enough, but we can't write more than a few notes on a page. Everything is sinister that was simple before. Showers are not showers. Stars are not stars.

We know there's still war, because we're near the RAF base, and there was the Falklands, and the kid whose uncle was killed, and we know there are starving kids covered in flies, but Africa's a different planet from here. We hear about an accident with a digger, where a builder's head got lopped clean off. They said it landed in the bushes on the playing field. We spend hours looking for it after school.

But children of the sea fear nothing. We grow up in the elements, on the cusp of life. One false step running down a cliff path. One freak gust out in the waves. One bad alley with a junkie tourist, one red-flag riptide, misjudged joyride, divebomb tuck-jump into rocks not sea.

A letter home to our parents, in that final term of school: 'Do not buy the Disney stickers from the men at the bus depot. These transfers are laced with LSD.'

Every term, we line up for worm milkshake. It is pink and thick and makes you puke. We think it's normal, until a new kid arrives whose family eats salad and someone says his parents have an ON-SWEET. When we tell him why we're queuing, he calls us pigs. We hold the milkshake in our cheeks then spit it out in the bogs. When our bums itch, we ignore it, and don't look for the squirming threads hanging out our pants.

3.

Mums go weird when you're eleven. Some of them seem happier they can treat us like friends. We stay up late watching TV with them. We pass their tobacco and watch them smoke.

Some mums seem suddenly sad. After telling us off, they cry, and pull us to their chests. We like the hug they give us, but wish at some point they'd let go.

Some mums still ignore us. They seem to be in shock they ever had us at all. We didn't know you could miss someone you see every day of your life.

You know which kind of mum you have by how they are when they pick you up from school. We secretly wish it was our mum at the front with her arms out, waiting to scoop us up, and because we're jealous, we call that kid Baby and make googoogaga sounds. Most of us in that final term make our own way home from school.

We are jealous of people with fathers, although we know there's only two types of men: the Ones Who Have Gone and the Bastards. Sometimes the Bastards go, but then they come back, and that's how you know.

There are too many types of women. We aren't sure which one we will be. After school, we go to the newsagents and gaggle around the magazines. We do the quizzes with yes/no arrows and follow the answers to find out.

We know there are strong women, like Margaret Thatcher, and we've done Elizabeth I at school. Elizabeth had no husband or children. Strong women must be alone.

In the summer holidays, mums stop liking us. They walk around in a kind of mist that repels you if you come too close. It's the summer they don't finish their sentences because they're so busy rushing, even when they're standing still.

There's only work when there's tourists, and there's only tourists when there's sun, so summers mean back-to-back shifts at two jobs – hotels for breakfast service or chambermaiding, then café work or shops, then back to hotels or restaurants for dinner shifts, or late nights working in pubs and clubs. They press their uniforms with the ironing board between us and each hiss and spit of it keeps us away.

We wish we could go to work instead of them so they could just sit in front of the TV. We get up in the night and crawl into bed with them. In the morning, they are gone.

4.

Some of us have kid siblings so we still know how good it feels just to play. All our old toys are passed on to them and we engineer ways to claim them back. To brush the long hair of our Barbie again, or push the head of our Ghostbuster figure so his eyes pop out.

It's the start of nostalgia, but we don't yet know that. If we did, we could explain the waves of violence that possess us when the little kids don't play how we want. When they grab back the Barbie or Ghostbuster, we thump them, over and over again. We see how big our hands are, on their throats, their wrists, their mouths.

There's a deliciousness in that violence, a bit like the hand you press over your pants at night. It lives in the same place, inside us, and it keeps us going back in for more. The violence becomes our secret and the little kids never tell. We know that love and pain go together. Men can hit women and the women still love them. Parents can beat you, but they still love you, and you love them, no matter what that woman from the charity said at school.

We still share baths with our younger siblings. We stretch out our bodies, leaving them cramped beneath the taps. We reach out our toes and prod them between their legs. We know things they don't know about their bodies. This knowledge increases us, somehow. We know that if we wanted to, we could tell them, and it would crush them, like a snail under a shoe.

We know what it's like, to be that snail, just as we know what it's like to be the shoe. You're the shoe when you're all in the gang together, firing water pistols at tourists from the car-park wall. But you're the snail when there's no one to hang out with, and you find yourself walking around town on your own, and everyone looks older and cooler than you, or you see a nice normal family on holiday, both parents smiling, holding their kids' hands.

You're the snail when Johnny says Robbie wants to get off with you, and you let him, and he pushes his hand inside your shirt, and you think of the diagrams on the blackboard, and how the diagram of your body had a space between its legs, and how the teacher said it was like a jigsaw, but you don't want to be a jigsaw, and you want Robbie to stop.

5.

We know our town is beautiful, because of the postcards we spin round on their shop carousels. But we have always known never to trust beautiful. When we were little, we fed the ducklings at the boating-lake then watched as seagulls snatched them up. Sometimes they dropped them. Either way, they died.

At some point, you have to choose to be a duckling or a gull.

We are the year group that gets British Bulldog banned, because we don't stop charging till blood gets spilt. The netball court at breaktime, fifty on one side, fifty on the other, glaring dagger-eyes before the charge. Waiting. Animals still throb in us. We want to hunt and kill.

The teachers want us to be nice like normal children so they decide to trust us with pets. Only animals can motivate us, because we are half animal ourselves. We name them after Streetfighter characters and, when no one's looking, we make them brawl.

We start with four guinea pigs, six rats and three gerbils. They live in cages, stacked on top of each other, and stink. The white rats all get cancer. Their death is very slow.

We hang out at the estuary, in a line on the bridge where the crabs cling onto weed. We own that bridge with our bare legs swinging and we don't let anyone through. We stab sandworms on the hooks of our crabbing lines and drop them in then wait for the tug. Adults say we have to throw the crabs back in again, but we hold them in our fingers and rip off their legs. Only then do we throw them in again, and watch their carcasses bob in the tide.

If America has a hurricane, the waves come back to us skyscraper high, and when the tide pulls back, it leaves a beach full of jellyfish, purple and big as plates. We take run-ups and jump down hard on them. The purple squidge splurts up. Slimy toes in fishy wet jelly guts. We do it for hours, till they all are dead.

One of the boys gets done for tying barbed wire round a seagull's throat. He was throwing it around and swinging it. The person who caught him thought he had a kite.

Life comes. Life goes. Children of the tide can never be devout.

6.

We know we're Cornish, because our school motto is in Cornish, and we're taught all the myths and traditions and old songs. Bussed out on school trips to tin mines and Tintagel, to the white stone Huer's Hut out on the cliff. They tell us how the Huer would sit here, looking for pilchards that once made our town. We take biros off the clipboards and, when nobody's looking, scrawl our legacy all over the walls. Robbie carves his name with a flick knife, so he'll always be here, when we're dead as the pilchards, dead as the tin.

But we know we're not Cornish. We weren't born here. We arrived. The only town cheap enough for our parents to begin again. We're betrayed by our accents, by mispronouncing place-names. It's *Gunarven* not Goon-haven, *Lanson* not Launces-ton, *Mowzel* not Mousehole (and there are no mice).

The old people call us Foreigners or Blow-ins. No different from the rubbish dragged in by the tide. They blame us for the way the town's changing. Not a quiet little picturesque fishing town, or a nice safe family resort. There's an airport now. People fly here for a tenner: hens, stags, students and underage teens, to get trashed to unconsciousness, sleep with strangers and leave with bad tattoos.

The old shops close. The cinema's boarded. Nightclubs, pound shops, piercing joints pop up. The theatre's a theme pub. A strip club opposite Woolworths.

Bouncers, not policemen, keep us safe.

We know we're not Cornish, but why would we want to be. There's nothing here but old stuff and seaweed and crap. Cornwall's like the dead leg you get from sleeping wrong. Come south of Plymouth and the world's blood cuts off.

All we want is to be older, and when we're older, we'll be gone. If we stay here, we will rot, like all the adults, like our mums, working for tips from tourists in this happy town of sad mistakes.

7.

We are old enough to be reckless, but not yet old enough to be wrecks. We line up on the harbour wall and dive into the water. We cannonball off clifftops and excavate caves. We surf all year round, weeing in our wetsuits to warm up in winter, pummelled by twenty-foot-high hurricane waves that snatch our breath and snap our boards. We're thrown into the shallows, laughing, suffocating, then turn around and go back in for more.

We crave it, that feeling of aliveness. We know we are immortal. Only we can cheat death.

We live in a land that holds freedom hard. Rebellion has always been the Cornish way. Not a county, the teachers tell us, but a dukedom — always owned, never ruled. Tinners and fishermen with no bosses. No one has served anyone here since time began.

We've been free to roam the town without adults for years now. We have a map of our kingdom: kissing spots, crying spots, where to get free food. We know the secret beach no one else goes to and how to read the tide so we can slip inside tunnels without getting cut off.

Vicky's mum works in the chippy and we badger her for batter bits that fall off the cod. When it rains, we trail the arcades, bugging the older kids for coppers, which we slide inside coin-slots to make more tumble out.

We know it's our last summer of freedom. Next year, we'll be waitressing, pot-washing, chambermaiding, scrubbing clots of ketchup off cheap plates. Soon, we'll work more hours than we're at school. We'll learn to hitch our skirts high and pull our tops low to get more tips than our mums. The women we work with will hate us. The world they are stuck in, we are merely passing through.

We'll find boyfriends in nightclubs, the older the better, and smoke weed in their bedsits and our cherries will pop. We will have our hearts broken. We will fight with our parents. Some of us will get pregnant. Some expelled. Some drop out. Meanwhile, the kids below us will steal our perfume and bras. They'll come to us with lovebites. We'll dab concealer on their boasts and regrets.

But this summer, our last summer before senior school, is like a trampoline that sends us whooping into the sky, still certain that the net will catch us, before sending us flying back up. We want to stay forever at that high point – arms and legs starfished, elation twisting our mouths, long hair all over the place, shirts blown above our heads. Stay forever, in that split giddy second, where bodies and boyfriends and work don't exist.

It's like the disposable cameras we get for birthdays. The things you want to hold on to forever are only blurs.

8.

The end of summer comes. The longest summer we've ever known. The same song was at number one in the charts the whole holidays and it messed up our sense of time. How brief it is, between knowing everything and knowing nothing. Between feeling so big, then becoming very small.

Come Monday, we'll be wearing our new uniforms. This is our last weekend. We go down to the beach on Saturday, weaving round the last of the fires and raves. Next week, the tourists will be gone, leaving rockpools full of beer cans and chunks of polystyrene boards.

We walk the beach, separate at first. A pack of boys. A gaggle of girls. Adam picks up a rubber johnny and throws it at us so the boys all laugh. Rob climbs the stack with the pink house on top of it, but the barbed wire's still there so he can't reach the bridge.

We sit in the cave that's too far for tourists. We're not afraid of the incoming tide. The kid from the RAF base sets up a Ouija board. Dark children need dark magic. It spells out D-I-E. Someone brings vodka. We pass it round. It looks like water but tastes like fire. Things will never be what they seem.

There are shriekings and bitchings and fumblings, then the moon comes out and turns the light on over the sea. We leave our cave when it's too cold to stay there. We dance back to the beach with our shadows on the sand.

Some go home. Most of us don't. We lie on our backs and make sand angels with our limbs. Some of us lie closely, hand in hand. Some of us kiss and pretend it's nice.

If we let ourselves, we can remember when it was okay to like things. When we let money-spiders run through our fingers, sending out webs we didn't break. When our noses dipped the surface of rockpools and we didn't grab at crabs we could pull out and rip.

There was a time once when little things amazed us. That first year of primary school, we lay with our heads in the hopscotch squares, and Leanne Petherson showed us her magic power of raising her hand to block out the sun. She said she first got the power with a lampshade. But now she can block out any light, if she tucks in her thumb. We all had a go. No big deal. We all turned the sun off. Leanne didn't speak to us for a week. When she cried in the toilets, we passed our tuck-shop buns under the door.

We'll be twelve soon. Dizzy, we look seawards. Lights on the fishing boats, and on the harbour walls. We raise our arms, and turn all the lights out with our small massive old young hands.

In the Pith

You're eleven, and smell of satsumas, which you rub on yourself on the bus. You pull up the sleeves of your oversized blazer and scrub the peel into your skin. You hold the segments and squeeze them lightly, daubing the juice on your face, your neck.

You're eleven, and smell of satsumas, because it has come to your attention there's a hierarchy in smell. And because there's a hierarchy, there's also betrayal. There's a right smell and wrong smell, and you mustn't smell wrong.

You don't know your own smell. You've tried, it's impossible. You haven't hit puberty, you don't even sweat. But smell is a collage of habitats and habits. A person's smell is not adjectives, but nouns. The nouns that make them: their homes, beds, parents, their hobbies, their bodies, their meals and routines.

You know your nouns, and your nouns are not their nouns. There's a gulf in your noun-ness: they are rich, you are poor. So you sit on the bus (noun) that smells of dirt (noun) and cigarettes (noun) and hope this satsuma (noun) will out-power the rest.

Satsumas are the scent of deception. The desperate scent of hoping you'll fit in.

You're eleven, in a kilt and starched blazer, because you go to posh school, not the comp in the town. The last year of primary was the year of clairvoyancy, when adults – school teachers, dance teachers, music teachers – were possessed by visions of what you should be.

Not your women though. They imposed no plan on you. They nested your youness like a precious bright egg, no urgency or pressure to hatch you, no fear of what creature may be growing inside. The teachers' vision, that you'd get a scholarship to the private school, didn't sit comfortably with them in this nest. It was everything they'd protested against, voted against, resented, a symbol or crucible for everything that was wrong.

How easy it is, when things are abstract. How difficult when the choice comes to your door. What is best for your child? What is best for society? A phrase you remember overhearing at this time: *If you can't change the system, make the best of the system.*

No harm just sitting the exam.

Your mother made you a special outfit for the interview, a chambray dress with a matching floppy hat, her sewing machine the soundtrack to wrestling her conscience. Thirty years later, she'll still ask if she did the right thing.

95

Your satsuma is political, but you don't yet know that. You don't know you are the subject of heated parliamentary debate. You don't know you're one of the last Assisted Places Scheme kids, manifesting Thatcher's vision of elite education for the gifted poor. The Tories call the scheme 'a ladder of opportunity'. Others call it 'cream-skimming', 'educational apartheid', a Dickensian handout, helping a few join the few.

The satsumas, like everything, are a gift from the Tories. Your new stiff uniform, your bus fare, too. Your school trips and school clubs and school fees and lunches, from which you sneak satsumas for this routine. But you're eleven, and small, and all this is beyond you. You're afraid you smell poor, and they'll tell.

What smells did you know before this?

Your home stretch of sea on a blustery day. The fish-guts harbour. Chip fat. Beans. The inside of old books. Your father's tobacco. Your ballet shoes. Josticks. Irn-Bru.

The dusty blush of paper-bag penny sweets. Silky soap pearls in birthday baths. Bread dough in your mother's floured fingers. Amber rosin crumbling on your violin bow.

Sunday tripe boiling for Toby-Dog. The nappy bags they used when you threw up. The smell of your gran's house. Calor gas heaters. Cloves at Christmas, making pomanders with your mum. Hot-water-bottle rubber in winter, and hot blackcurrant and vapour rub when you were ill.

The smell in the grotty bar your dad ran for a while that seeped upstairs into the flat where you all briefly lived. The stench of the old woman's house your mum cleans, urine, mould and milk. Banana Nesquik (good) and banana-flavour antibiotics (bad). Sweet, rank Worm Medicine Milkshake, the vilest smell of all.

But your home had no smell. Your mum had no smell. And you had no smell.

Until now.

On your first day of school, you breathed them in – these posh, pretty children, as fragrantly perfect as a wedding bouquet. Stood as close as you dared in the lunch queue, to lean in and wonder at the scent of their hair. Picked up another kid's blazer by accident to inhale the fabric conditioner seeped into its seams. Walked through liberal sprays of changing-room deodorant, so you might smell of vanilla too.

Obsessed with fresh breath, like adverts or film stars, all the kids here munch mints or chew gum. You can't afford either, so you secretly eat toothpaste, sneaking licks of it at break in the loo.

Satsumas look identical on the outside. It takes a long time for bad insides to show. That's what you all are, then, those first weeks of posh school: a bowl of satsumas with matching veneers, waxy and radiant, peels intact, new.

But you knew before you came here your insides were different. Your fear is how long before they all know too. Later, a boy will say you smell of biscuits. You'll want to die right there in the hall.

You're eleven, bone-jangled on the school bus, a knot of dread growing in your guts. You're shivering with cold, knees tucked up inside your blazer, a boxy boys' blazer, because until recently it was an all-boys school. Girls like you are slowly arriving, but a century of tradition is slow to turn round.

You watch through the window as the dark turns to dawn, as the coast turns to moorland to villages and farms, the old bus battling steep hills and blind-corners, the knot of dread growing the closer you get.

After an hour and a half, you reach the outskirts of the city, and the dread turns to vomit in your throat. Kids pile on at each estate stop, not kids from your school but the comp up the road. When they see your uniform, they hurl abuse at you. Sometimes they throw sandwiches. Once a can hit your head.

You make yourself small and pretend to read quietly. The jeering lasts until your stop.

You want to say: *Look! I'm not posh! I'm the same as you! In fact I'm probably way below you! I'm not one of them! I'm one of you!*

But you aren't one of them either. You aren't one of anyone. Your old obsession with categories kicks in. At eleven, as at five, the world is confusing. Again, this hopscotch between boxes, tossing stones into squares and hoping you'll land safe.

The new school is a riddle of categories. You must observe intently to make order emerge.

In the first days, it's easy: Boy/Girl, Day-Kid/Boarder, English/ Foreign, Cool/Clever, Quiet/Loud.

You reduce the boys into labels by hobby: Rugby, Skater, Warhammer, IT. The girls are trickier – partly because there's so few of them, and partly because girls in general have never made sense to you – but you identify Bitches, Bookworms and Boy-Chasers, with differentiators including skirt length, bra type, pony ownership, smoking, make-up and netball skills.

The original division – the one you'd arrived with – the simple binary of them rich/you poor – turns out to be the most complex category. There is wealth and there is status – kids of aristocrats and celebrities, kids of long local landowning lineage, the nouveau riche kids with fake cockney accents and flashy tuck- shop cash. There are children with parents in the Armed Forces, and children sent over from Hong Kong, arriving with no language except *Hello* and *Happy Birthday* and given antique English names. Kids sent at five to boarding school, seeing their farflung parents a few weeks a year. Families who'd scraped everything they could together, sacrificed and saved, to send their kids to a good school.

There are kids who think they're poor but still go skiing. Kids on various scholarships for music or sport. You only know one other kid with a single mother. You don't know if anyone else is on the same scheme as you, but you're sure you must be the worst off on paper. You conceal this fruit inside you, and focus on the peel.

The structure of a satsuma is symmetrical. The segments near identical. All peel the same. The uniqueness of each individual is to be found in its pith pattern, as erratic as capillaries, a haphazard embroidery of disordered threads. The stuff you pick off and discard, unwanted. Scientific name *mesocarp* – *meso*: middle, in-between.

Satsuma is the smell of your between-ness. Neither one thing nor the other. The pith between the two. Grafting the veneer of this new school-you onto the sweet fruit of your family, your inside-you.

It takes a long time to discover the truth of a satsuma. They mask their inside so long and so well. No way to tell from the outside if they're sweet or bitter, shrivelled or lush.
You have to get close to know its secrets. Unpeel it. Taste it. Only then do you know.

Weeks become months, strangers become friends, and playdates and sleepovers begin. The discomfort of visiting these big posh houses is worth it for the invitation to shower in their en suite. You only have a bath at home, often second-hand water. In these new friends' showers, you try every bottle on display, toiletries so sumptuous you don't even understand the labels. You hope the concoctions will seep into you in layers, embalming you into this unlived life.

Sleepovers bring intimacy and secrets. Children need the dark to share their dark. In midnight confessionals, between smuggled sweets and who-do-you-fancy, your classmates slowly unpeel.

You discover – beneath the holidays, the horses and cleaners, the spas and the ski trips, the peacocks on the lawn – beneath the acres and nannies and brand-full wardrobes – beneath the double-barrel lacquer and words like *Mumsy, supper, Pops* – beneath the peel, when you get to the pip and pith of them – you discover you are, all of you, the same.

All of you – all of us – confused half-children. Bruiseable, bully-able, vulnerable, afraid. All holding our peel, else our insides betray us. Just atoms in robes, and beneath the robes, hurt.

You write in your diary: *I thought I'd be the messed-up one. But in reality I'm really not.*

Your friends love coming, when you eventually let them, to your house. Your home might be small but the love is vast. They love your mum, the safety and warmth in your zanily painted kitchen where they can sit on the counter and talk without judgement and laugh and cook wholesome food, bread and pasta and ice cream from scratch. The freedom of spending hours on the beach, collecting shells to make necklaces. The freedom of being accepted, without pressure or pretence.

Friendships are forged in the unpeeling of those moments. Then you go back to school and sew your outsides back on.

You like peeling satsumas. You like picking off the pith. You pretend you're a surgeon, with careful tweezers, nimbly unravelling the white threads with no rip. You don't eat the pith, but your mum says it's healthy. Full of nutrients. Where the goodness is.

You learn that pith comes from the Old English for *substance*. Substance is a word used a lot at this school – in the brochure, in assemblies, in school reports. *People of substance, a man of great substance, a young woman of substance.* The more you hear it, the less it makes sense. In Chemistry, in Physics, substance means 'matter'. The tangible is-ness of a physical thing. In ideas or debates, it means seriousness, validity.

Aren't we all matter, with is-ness, with validity? Don't we all have substance – not because of our school?

It takes a while for you to show your *substance*. To shrug off your peel and revel in your pith. To own your between-ness, your validity, your is-ness, in this world of identical peels.

Individuality requires groupthink to push against. You cultivate non-conformity. The Art of Pith. Tweak the uniform. Dare eccentric hairstyles. Rebel in quiet but significant ways. You sing hymns backwards in chapel and refuse to say Amen. You develop a radar for underground anarchy, sniffing out like-minded teachers and peers. Those in the system, but not of the system. Inside-outsiders, in English, in Drama, in Art.

You don't break rules, but you work within them to mock them. At fourteen, you have to give a careers presentation. Told that first a dancer, then an actor, then a writer, aren't 'proper jobs', you deliver a rigorously researched talk on being an undertaker instead.

When your form tutor complains to your mother about your unconventional hair, your mother looks the teacher firmly in the eye and says, quietly but assertively, a line so perfect it could have come from a film:

> My daughter does everything that is asked of her here
> and more, with diligence and grace and hard work,
> and if she chooses to express her individuality through
> her hairstyle then I don't believe anyone is in a posi-
> tion to judge.

How did you get here? You certainly didn't ask for it. How did you end up in this shiny-peel world?

You'd been walking down a road, a one-way road, with all your classmates, in that final year of primary school. A road of we-hood, cornerlesss, bendless, a nice straight road you didn't even think about, you just walked. You thought you'd keep on walking, all of you together, to a known place ahead.

And then suddenly – a junction. Two new roads, left and right of you. Posh school one way. Ballet school the other. And the rest of them kept walking, as adults ushered you away from them. At eleven, with no consciousness on your part, their projection of your futurehood led you elsewhere, the phantom of your adult-self tugging your child-hand.

What would have happened if you'd stayed on that straight road to state school? What kind of pupil, of girl-woman, would you have become? You'd have worked just as hard. You'd have got the same grades. You'd have had sleepovers in houses like yours. You wouldn't have got the bus. Wouldn't have worried about smelling wrong. Perhaps that early we-hood, that sense of belonging, would have stayed intact.

But still, you'd have found something to push against. In any school you went to, you wouldn't have fitted in. You had always been Other, in other ways, even in primary school. Posh school simply gave Otherhood a tangible skin.

Pith gets thicker and darker with age. More pronounced. More visible. Impossible to ignore. You brazenly inhabit the pith of you, as those seven years of school drag on. As injustice, in all forms, becomes clearer. As discomfort grows deeper that you are part of this world.

Private education is a conspiracy of language. Exclusivity bound in the manacles of names – *Prep*, not homework; *Quad*, not playground; *Supper*, *Prefects*, *Dawson*, *Sir*. Latin mottos, like laws of nature, affirming the power of tradition: 'This is always how it was'.

'This is always how it was' – wealth begets better education, begets careers and cultural capital, begets good marriages, begets more wealth.

'This is always how it was' – systemic abuse in the boarding house, brutal initiations around school, blood on a boy's pants when they were ripped off over his head by a baying mob of sixth-formers – 'This is always how it was'. You raise it with the teachers, who shrug and dismiss it. You refuse a prefectship to make a point.

'This is always how it was'. The same applied to your world – violence begets violence begets violence. Cycles of poverty, addiction, abuse.

'This is always how it was'. What lazy shorthand to keep people, of all classes, of all backgrounds, in a cage.

Time went on. Green mould gathered on the veneer of your education, rotting from within as satsumas do. They sagged and stank, your school days. That plump robustness gone. The insides leaked, and you understood.

It wasn't money. It wasn't class. It wasn't status. It was something about story. About power and truth.

You and your family wrote your own story. You felt sorry for your classmates with weighty tomes imposed on them. Stories pre-written, desperately clung to, roles allocated. Your school was no better and no worse than any other. It just had the money to tell its story with spin.

You came to see class not as a hierarchy, or ladder, but as two revolving doors, circling endlessly, side by side. Processions of children, unhappy in their own ways, forced into circling without choice round and round.

Did I do the right thing, your mother still asks you.

Yes. Because she did away with doors. Revolving or otherwise. She made you doorless. There's always a different entrance. And a different way out.

Your brother got the last government assisted place two years later. He too felt the difference, but felt it differently from you. Perhaps it's no coincidence you both ended up with degrees in politics. Neither of you ended up with 'proper jobs'. Both of you *meso*, in the pith, both peel-less. Both of you doorless. You are who you are.

New Labour abolished the Assisted Place Scheme, which cost £800 million in its seventeen years. The money was diverted into Sure Start and early years provision for those in need. Here, again, you were a political statistic – the model for Sure Start was based on the community centre that rescued your family in your steel town years.

But for now, you are eleven, and you don't know any of this. You know you are different, you smell wrong, and you're cold, and your skirt is too long, and you don't wear a bra yet, and you don't want a sandwich to be hurled at your head.

A satsuma is an interconnected system. Tensile forces keep it together, keep it round. The push–pull pressure. The mesocarp mesh. Pith is responsible for wound repair. Pith is the healer, holding the whole.

Its smell comes from volatile compounds, organically colliding, the clash sparking sweet scent. You smell of this clash, of these volatile compounds, of the organic collision of things beyond your control.

The smell of a satsuma changes with its genetics, its conditions of development and its ripeness at harvest – as we ourselves change too. Later, you'll feel ashamed of your private education. Ashamed to acknowledge that it might have been a ladder after all. But you can't hide it, and you mustn't. In spite of it, or because of it, you are who you are.

To be the peel is to hide what's inside you. The truth of us, the power of us, the goodness, the healing, lies in the pith.

You stuff the remnants of the fruit in your pocket, keep your head down past the other kids, and get off the bus. It's a long walk up to school, bag and mind heavy. By the time you get there, you won't smell of satsumas. You'll smell of rain. You'll smell unknowably of you.

The Girl Who Read Woolf

She arrived as a gift from your teacher, in a box of ten books with a card. You knew you were destined to love her, although you had tried – and failed – in the past.

A gift from a teacher – like you, an outsider, in this linear, straitjacket school. His classroom was a jungle of houseplants, his mind mercurial, his knowledge vast. He treated you like adults. He had studied at Oxford and travelled the world. You saw him as a lighthouse, circling dark–light–dark, illuminating the rocks on which you felt you might wreck. Offering safe passage through the perilous seas of teenhood, to the shores of adulthood unmarked on your map.

He set your compass through conversations in his garden about literature, politics, writing and art. Through educational mixtapes: Roberta Flack, Laurie Anderson, Romanian madrigals, Bob Dylan, Nick Drake. Through experimental theatre, his controversial school plays – you were Winnie in Beckett's *Happy Days*; Juliet, kissing a much younger Romeo; the single mother in *Top Girls*; a Myra Hindley-esque witch in *Into the Woods*, slabs of butcher's meat dripping over the stage.

So when he gave you these books – a box of Modern Classics, bound in cellophane, beautiful, brand new – you felt he was rolling out a map. He was saying: Look up! Let these books be Polaris, charting your way through the dark.

She arrived in a box with nine men. You read them first, because their names were more famous: Kafka, Márquez, Orwell, Steinbeck, others you can't remember now. You devoured the men in the first weeks of summer. How extravagant it had felt, to read books so new. Sacred, almost, to be the very first to touch them, to smell them, to break their spines. You had felt like Howard Carter, Neil Armstrong, Columbus, the first into brave new worlds.

You left her till last, because you didn't like the front cover. But mainly because you were afraid. You wanted to love her. You craved an awakening. You wanted to be the Girl Who Read Woolf.

You had a thing for suicidal women. You sought dark idols for your heart. Sylvia Plath. *Hamlet*'s Ophelia. Juliet, of course. Madame Bovary, Anna Karenina. Antigone, in her cell. The power, the boldness, the strength of it, the perverse tragic majesty of taming the untameable: Death.

You had known that compulsion, at the start of that summer. Near breaking, not yet broke.

She arrived as a gift and you took her to the harbour, with your torch, and an apple and pen, and fifty pence for the payphone in case you needed to call home. You were working as a waitress that summer, as you had done every summer since you were thirteen, and there were a few hours between lunch and dinner shifts in which you would escape to the harbour to read.

You had a cave of one's own – too hidden for tourists, too high for toddlers, too small for the gangs of teens roaming the town. For years, it had been your reading spot, this dank cracked cranny with the fishy wet floor, sitting on the thick beam of wood wedged into it that used to moor boats, an old chain twisted around still, rusting and heavy with barnacles and salt.

Your run-down town didn't have a lighthouse, but the book was set in Cornwall. This would surely be your Woolf.

You began. It felt stale. Too Victorian. Mrs this, Mr that. Slow, heavygoing, no plot to it. A trapped posh wife and a domineering man. This wasn't your Cornwall: a big house, easels, servants, French dishes, lawns. It belonged to the shiny veneer of your school world. Where was the pith?

You broke your rule of never reading a book twice (because there were too many books to read as it was). Got to the end, returned, began again. If you couldn't find your Cornwall, you might find yourself instead.

Because wasn't that what you were doing that summer? Looking for yourself in every woman you met. In every book, every film, every song lyric. In shops, both the cashiers and customers. In the raucous hen parties staggering round town.

In the matriarchy of the restaurant, in the women you worked with, worked for, served. The owner's daughter, tanned, tall and curvy, so confident, independent, so self-assured, who had dropped out of school and had a boyfriend in his thirties, and they drove around together in his orange MG. You wanted to be her, staring at her with wonder, wishing yourself into her, but you knew you never could.

You could never be the owner's beautiful strong daughter because you were broken, or made the wrong way.

Woolf was broken too. She was not a normal woman. If you could fall in love with her, decipher her, learn her, you might fall in love with, decipher, yourself.

The second time you read it, July turned rainy. Your cave walls were dripping and you took a towel for your bench. You lay on your belly, legs bent on the rockface, Woolf propped against the craggy wall. After an unusually high tide, the floor was carpeted with dogfish, seaweed, mermaid's purses and pecked-apart crabs, so that the smell of her writing became salty and harboury, and when you opened it again at nighttime, you were still by the sea.

The third time, you let yourself write in it, breaking another self-imposed rule. Underlined passages, circled words or phrases, used the margins to identify metaphors and themes.

To understand Woolf, you had to learn to be a rule-breaker. Transgression is integral to rites of passage when you're young. You did another thing too, for the first time – you read some to yourself, very quietly, out loud.

And slowly, like an old-fashioned courtship, paragraph by paragraph, page by page, there came love.

The door to Woolf opened and you ran through it giddy. Read everything in the library. *The Waves* was your book. You couldn't write in it, it was borrowed, but you didn't need to, the cipher now set in your bones. A frequency – that's what Woolf was. A frequency, like they say granite has on the moors. Let yourself shed everything, tune into it, and you feel her bones in your bones.

Sometimes, you felt her slip into you, or you into her, like you had a new skin. Sometimes, when swimming, you pretended you were drowning, but peacefully, rocks in your fists. When you wrote in your diary, it was her hand not your hand. You and her, interchangeable, like any first love.

What comes first – being broken or being isolated? Certainly, that summer, you were both.

Your best friend, your anchor, had moved back to Japan. Your peers in the town went drinking and clubbing. Your schoolfriends were off on long foreign holidays. In a place heaving with people, you had never felt more alone.

You moved like a stranger through the streets of your home. You didn't want to be there. You felt you would rot. You told your mother you were *a chronological refugee*. You bought Victorian nightgowns in charity shops and wafted round clifftops and beaches barefoot, long hair blowing, collecting hagstones for necklaces, thinking about life, about love, about womanhood, writing tortured poetry, picking your skin till it bled.

This was how to deal with not-belonging: cultivate solipsism. Make it an art.

In the restaurant that summer, you met an artist. He reminded you of your teacher – well-travelled, well-read; insightful; cultured; storied; rolling out another piece of map for your life. His studio was in the old Victorian lifeboat station, teetering on a promontory at the far end of the cliffs. He asked you to model for a painting of Ophelia. You posed for him once a week.

The studio was magical – dark, salty, shadowed, music playing from a mezzanine, Delibes, Debussy, Philip Glass, scaffolds and platforms and canvases and tableaus, a Calor gas heater, glowing blue, for the drafts. He painted traditionally, studying the Old Masters, mixing his own oil paints, painting everything from life. Meticulous, laboursome, devotional translation of reality into art.

You stayed so still, trying hard to be inanimate, trying to quell the excitement of this new role of yours, this thrill. Masking, often failing to mask, the surges of electric energy that newly jostled through your bones. Posing as a dead woman, you had never felt more alive. The conversations you had with him, cross-pollinating concepts, creating connections between disparate things, the rigorous debates and provocative questions, the intellectual interrogation of the self, of the world. Trying to lie still, with your synapses dancing. The challenge of silence when he was drawing your mouth. You felt he would need a new canvas, as each time he painted you, you grew and grew.

He was the first person to read your writing, to make you keep writing, to believe in the purpose of your craft. You would pose for him for the next ten years, the paintings a chronicle from schoolgirl, to girl-woman, to university student, a companion to your diary in flesh.

The more you found yourself in art, in ideas, in Virginia, in glimpses of adult worlds beyond your grasp, the less solid your present self became. Like *Henry V* again, that film with your gran, when all that was around you in that moment dissolved. Only this time, you were in a hole with no ladder. Nothing could be fixed, made solid, any more.

Life was a difficult thing that summer, which you often thought might be your last. It was hot, the tourists pink-peeling, the sun was relentless, but all you saw was dark. Dark in the restaurant, as you served up pizza, dark at home where you retreated to your room, dark in your bed where you'd lie for hours staring, and suddenly, inexplicably, cry, cry, cry.

It was extravagant that darkness. An indulgence. Romantic, how you'd lie there thinking of death, how you'd step off a curb to see if cars would swerve or hit. Nostalgic, to have your mother sit by your bedside, as you rejected her soft soothing words. The melodrama of burying your head in your her lap and sobbing, I'm alone, I'm all alone.

The pageantry of pain you paraded that summer. Your self-obsessed poetry, tense with pity and pastiche. Sometimes, you got crippling headaches which you described to the doctor as a head full of bees.

You stopped reading. Craved sleep, which was elusive. Stayed up all night playing clock patience, or watching old Westerns, then crying, then staring at the ceiling, ripping the skin off your lips, till they bled so much you were nearly unconscious and daubed the blood on your notebook next to quotes from Woolf, Plath, Keats.

What would your death matter. Nothing mattered. Nothing was solid. Nothing was real. Everything was pointless. You were pointless. An insignificant, lonely broken girl.
Everything was breaking or broken. The world, the news, all getting worse.

You felt the pain of everyone in the world that summer. When you feel like someone you become them. You had known that since you were young. You were drawn to others' pain like iron filings to a magnet. Maybe seeking tangible legitimacy for your own. Your hurt, nameless and unnameable, desperately needed a source. You cut out photos from newspapers of wars, famines, massacres, sad faces, dead faces, faces covered in blood. When you couldn't sleep, you listened to the World Service, despatches from crises in every corner of the Earth.

What could you do about the mess of it? Nothing. And it would go on like this, until the end of the world. The conflict, the cruelty, the wickedness. The men and the men and the men.

By August the town was busier than ever – the best place in the world to see the total eclipse. Cornwall's hopes were pinned on the moment when the sun would fall from the sky. Every hotel and hostel past capacity. Campsites heaving. Touts flogging merchandise on every street.

How long this town had milked the sun for quick riches. Now there'd be no sun, it would milk the dark.

The day before, a quarter of a million tourists congested the one road into Cornwall. Garages ran out of petrol. Beer bought like the last day on earth. The county prepared for carnage. Water bowsers ready in case taps ran dry. Police standing by for hedonism. Camera crews setting up for broadcasts on the day.

You didn't need to see the eclipse. You'd become one.

Ten days earlier, you'd failed to die.

The eclipse had been weighing on you heavily. A sense of fore-boding had been triggered in your bones. You were troubled by it coming, its portent. That summer, you were trying to divine meaning from all things. Writing in the margins of life, sieving for significance, seeking metaphors and themes.

The newspapers were full of eclipse talk. You read and you read and you read.

How Chippewa people shot flaming arrows into the sky to restart the sun, believing it had snuffed out. How the Babylonians put fake kings on the throne to keep the real one safe. How Aztec women hid their pregnancies, believing a great beast would eat their babies if they watched. How astrologers in ancient China were executed if they failed to protect the emperor by not predicting an eclipse. In Japan, they covered their wells to stop poison raining down from the sky. In India, they immersed themselves in rivers, to escape the fire dragon swallowing the world.

People like you, across cultures and centuries, trying to create narratives to make phenomena make sense. The eclipse coming now was explainable. Science – that's all. No threat, no trick. It was everything else that made no sense to you. How to think, how to be, how to live.

Eleventh of August, eleven a.m. Your family, excited, joined the town on the cliffs. You'd trailed behind them moodily for five minutes, then turned around abruptly and stomped back home. Rejecting the eclipse was rejecting belonging – to your family, to your town, to the world. A rejection of rapture, awe and wonderment. Of the idea that anything could be bigger than yourself.

But *eclipse* comes from the Greek for 'being abandoned'. Back at home, under your blankets, you felt a pang, which shook you out your self-absorbed stupour and sent you running in a panic out the house.

You would see it. You must see it. You'd be with them. All that mattered was to be with them on the cliffs. You ran and ran – but look up, was this it? – the sky a vengeful rumble of purpling dark – and no one around you, shops shut, no traffic – it was happening – you were too late, too late –

You stood still, panting. You would have to watch it here. Where were your eclipse glasses? If you didn't wear them, you'd go blind.

You ran again, homewards, eerie air, streets deserted, running through the day that was fast becoming night. The front door had locked itself. You'd run out without thinking.

You sat on your garden wall. It was coming. You'd thought you'd missed it, but that had just been the start.

It was cloudy, and muggy, and drizzly, and dark with a fizziness, a creature-like dark, and the event of a lifetime – unmissable, ancient, connecting you to history, mythology, space – something so worthy of your attendance was happening, and while the world looked up you looked down at your feet.

Then – a light through the darkness. Not from above, but across the road. The house across the road, the bungalow. The neighbours were at home, watching the eclipse on TV.

So that's how you watched it, the event of a lifetime – squinting through curtains at a stranger's TV. The black disc of moon ate the white disc of sun. We all were extinct. The world was dead.

Then the day came back on. Cheers from the cliffs. It would not happen again for another ninety-one years.

That was it. Your chance. And you squandered it. How petty, how arrogant, to consume your own light.

You vowed –

> When they come home, I'll be happy. I'll hug them and say sorry for being a grump.

You promised yourself –

> From now on, I'll be different. I'm wasting myself and my life.

But your family came home and you didn't even look at them. They unlocked the door and you slumped off to bed.

You were sent to a counsellor that summer. She prattled on about her daughter. You barely said anything. You didn't go back.

You were sent to a psychiatrist, who left you to a student. You barely said anything. You didn't go back.

Your tongue was locked, but your diary was open. You wrote and wrote and wrote. You recorded your dreams like prophecies. Kept lists of world crises. Planned your own funeral, copied out quotes. You sketched your self-portrait, over and over, a twisted distortion of a Schiele-esque face.

That summer you were friendless, you found the greatest confidante, notebooks hearing and holding your despair.

> *'I think therefore I am' — so will I die if I stop thinking? I no longer want to think. I need a void, some empty space, that lets nothing else in . . . I am decaying, a silent process, a gradual process, no one can see, no one wants to see, no one can hear me rotting, but in my head exists a chaos I cannot refuse. When did I start hiding? I just want to be normal, I want to be free . . . I live as a fugitive, my world dark and cavernous, it twists and turns, I fall again and again.*

Your diary had a voice that spoke back in the second person, chastising your patheticness, telling you off:

> *Holly, you are not dying. You are not a refugee. Your family has not been ravaged by Chechan rebels or Zimbabwean electioneers. You are simply in turmoil. Your conflict is miniscule. Do not be a victim, for you are not one. Be satisfied. You have no right to be so despairing. No right.*

But then it could be gentle, coaxing, a therapist:

Why are you unhappy? Think about it Holly. You are angry. Why?

You replied to yourself:

Because I am human and that is the worst thing in this universe to be.

Near the end of the summer, a third person entered your pages. You had an inner-child session with a wise family friend. You could see your girl-self clearly, skipping through a field, red ribbons, white dress. You gifted your girl-self the safety of your diary, writing in the third person to, and about, her:

Little Holly had to hide. To cope with everything, she shut herself down, closed her face, closed her heart, became something else. She has layers like an onion, and I cry as I unpeel her, each more painful than the last. Do I impose Big Holly's thoughts on her? This strange hybrid creature: little body, two heads.

You had always known there were a thousand selves in your body. Your diary gave voice to them, let them all speak. It was something you did, still do, without thinking: IYouWeSheThey, all the same.

What did you do, the rest of that summer? You'd abandoned Woolf. Stopped reading altogether. Migraines, failure to concentrate, head too full to absorb any more. You worked sixty hours a week. Kept on smiling for tips. When you'd tried and failed to end it all, you slept for hours then still went to work. You were there, but not there. A robot in a dress.

Dead? No, I'm never dead. My greatest fear: I am always still alive.

It came – the void you'd longed for:

No thinking, no feeling, just numbness. Dead from the neck upwards, though the face still functions. I still smile when I take their orders, when I take their plates out, when I give them their bill. I watch myself do it, like watching a stranger, out of body, a spectator in my own skin. A physical entity with no mental existence.

I have died inside. My wish came true. How I wish that it hadn't. But now it's too late.

Too late, they say, you wanted to stop thinking, so we came in the night and took your brain. We took your brain, and you can't have it back, Little Girl. You're headless now. Too late.

September. You returned to school headless. You had wanted to return as the Girl Who Read Woolf.

Instead, you *were* Woolf. You didn't know it at the time, but you see it so clearly now. Now you've read all Woolf's diaries, and re-read your own. You see it so clearly, aged forty, that it hurts you. You want to hold tight to your teenage self.

You want to hold that hurting girl-woman, and let your tears wash her, baptise her anew. You want to say:

> Look! This life can be beautiful. Your life will be beautiful. You are beautiful. Hold on.

You want to say:

> Come. Sit. Let's talk a while. The night is warm and the sea is still. Sit. We'll say everything in nothing. Just feel my hand in your hand. Our two hearts, still going, keeping time like a clock.

You want to sit with your hurting girl-self and kiss the skin back onto her lips. To read Woolf's diaries, all five volumes, out loud to her, to prove to her that great art can come from this hurt. To read what Woolf felt when she witnessed an eclipse, so your girl-self can feel it and witness one too.

To say:

> I know you think you're a bundle of fractures. You have all these bits of you and can't make them whole. The Daughter, the Sister, the Schoolkid, the Dancer, the Teenager, the Little Lost Girl. You have been many people. There are many more to come. But look at us – we made it to forty! And forty is brilliant. We are finally whole.

It takes forty weeks to grow a baby. It takes forty years for a woman to grow. Forty: a birth, a renewal. Finally, boldly, joyfully, regretless and shameless, inhabiting our skin.

Look up, my girl. I am sun, you are moon. There's a sky we both live in, without eclipsing the light.

Hold on, my girl. You must keep going. Keep living. We must never give up.

Keep on keeping on, my girl. *Keep* – Old English, to seize, to care for, to attend. *On* – Greek for being, existing. Seize your existing. Attend to it. Care for your being for all that it's worth.

Keep onning, as I will keep onning, even when it feels impossible, when you want to give up. Keep onning, when death seems a solace, when there's too much life in life to live.

On, on, you must trust me, keep living, keep going now, on and on. Because one day you'll wake up, forty, a mother, and it will be terrifying to read in your girl-woman diary that once you thought so lightly, so indulgently, so longingly, so selfishly and pathetically, of death.

I C$_{43}$H$_{66}$N$_{12}$O$_{12}$S$_2$ You

The Mother and her children are eating dinner, lively chatter bouncing between the profound and the profane, when the eldest, on the cusp of his thirteenth birthday, announces:

I'm never having kids.

I'm not either, says his younger brother. Kids are annoying. I AM one so I know!

You'll have *loads* of children, the eldest teases. I'll be the fun uncle. With lots of dogs.

My grand-dogs? laughs the Mother.

Exactly!

As long as I don't have to look after them all, she says.

The boys bicker with disgust about procreation, unaware their bodies might one day wish to be shared. Their bodies are their bodies. Present tense. They own them. Bodies for diving, digging, climbing, in the now. Boys' bodies. Does that make a difference? No socialised expectation of giving, being given, given up.

125

I said the same once, admits the Mother. *I'm never having children.* I was adamant, just like you.

The Mother hasn't told them this before. Children need a sense of pre-existence to feel immortal, to feel they always existed, in thought, or dream. But they're old enough now, she thinks, to benefit from her narrative. To hear the tale of her becoming, the roles they played. To understand the future is never fixed, but flowing. The beautiful mutability that comes with age.

But now I have you guys, she says, and I wouldn't change it for anything.

Seriously?

Not for anything in the world.

The boys move on to some other conversation, the Mother reminding them to use cutlery, so that they suddenly seem so young again, mauling carrots with their hands.

When she was a girl, when the future was overwhelming, one thing was certain: she was never having kids.

Motherhood for her was never a destination. It wasn't even a stop on the way. Her upbringing smashed open stereotypes. In the world her women laid out for her, girls had strong shoulders, minds and legs. Princesses, in her bedtime stories, slew their own dragons and didn't need a prince. At nursery, her friends played Mummies and Daddies. She played Miners, Astronauts,

Explorers. She was a kid in dungarees and Doc Martens, who knew girls must never let anything hold them back.

She would tell everyone it was wrong to have children when so many children didn't have mums and dads. She turned her doll's house into an orphanage, the Playmobil parents all wicked or dead.

Literature was to blame for a lot of it. In all the books she read, mums never came off great. Either they died – the nice ones, usually – or they were evil. Or vague, distracted by housework, when their children were screaming about monsters under the bed.

Of all the women she knew, she wanted to be like her auntie, who had always been a kind of second mum. Her auntie-mum had lived with them, only a teenager when they were born, young and funny, joyful and warm. She made up the best stories, doing all the characters' voices, put on plays in the living-room, invented fun games. They'd get the art box out and paint pictures, gluey collages. Once she rescued a hedgehog off the road. She was the first family member to finish school and keep studying, moving to London, where they went to visit her all the time, going around Camden Market, trying jazzy hats on, eating canal-side jacket potatoes, watching buskers play. She was a beaming bright splatter-paint rainbow, who flung open a window into how the future could be. A new form of womanhood rolled out to you, boundless, brilliant, bold – art and literature and politics, feminism, veganism and animal rights, humour and affection, a career, independence, dyed hair, quirky cardigans, jazzy leggings, DMs.

Her niece vowed to be just like her. She would never have children. The single certainty in her uncertain world. So certain, that when the girls queued at primary school to be immunised against some disease they might pass on later in the womb, she refused to roll her sleeve and had a stand-off with the nurse.

> I don't need it, she stated defiantly. I'm never having kids.

The nurse plunged the needle in swiftly. The injustice hurt more than the jab.

But there was a man, and there was love, and there was a bucket list: 'Get pregnant' scribbled next to 'Run a marathon' and 'Write a novel' on the inside cover of her copy of Zelda and Scott Fitzgerald's letters.

She ran the marathon. Began the novel. Got pregnant.

And then the doubt and panic set in.

Pregnancy is 394,200 minutes of not knowing anything. She approached it like a war, or exam. She wanted all the intelligence she could gather. She wanted facts. She wanted knowledge and a plan. While her body grew larger – strangers asked if it was twins – she shrank her fears to an A4 folder, organised by trimesters and bullet-point lists.

The problem was, the words unnerved her. She used shorthand for words she hated in her notes. She refused to speak the language of her anatomy. The lexicon disgusted her, got stuck in her throat. She was ashamed of the words of her body. She had always felt more like a boy.

Her oldest friend, a nurse and mother, teased her, singing *Vagina vagina vagina*, down the phone. How ugly, how inaccurate – *Vagina*, meaning 'sheath for a sword'. *Womb* meaning 'bowels'. *Hymen*, the Greek god of marriage, with its etymology in 'bind' or 'sew'.

All her life, she had sewn silence around her womanhood. No wonder she'd vowed never to have children. She couldn't even face naming the machinery involved.

What comes first – hating your body or hating the words for that body? What would she rather these parts of her were called? Words that meant caves, shrines, holy places. Protective and protected, hiding treasure inside. The shelter in which girls become adults. No bowels. No marriage. No swords.

This is how you changed me, my firstborn: you opened my dictionary and erased the shame.

She was pregnant, she had knowledge, she now had language. But she was missing the main ingredient: love.

She knew love was missing because she was different from the women who stroked their bellies like heirloom teapots in the antenatal groups she loathed. Women flooding their unborns with adulation, repeating the teacher's mantras about the universe and love.

What was she missing? Why wasn't she like that? How can you love a person you've never even met?

The teacher said, *Talk to your babas.* Everyone did, out loud, except her.

I'm sorry you won't be born to one of these mothers. Of all the wombs of all the women in the world, you're stuck in mine.

She had a sense the baby didn't want to be in there either. It moved around constantly. Never lay still. So many somersaults it gave itself hiccups. Too restless to tell them its gender, the one fact she needed, in the scans. But she was restless too.

> You just need to relax a bit, someone told her. When you're calm, baby's calm.

Knowledge was normally calming. But for the first time, knowledge was not enough.

She studied a book about the chemical oxytocin. The 'love' hormone, underpinning attachment, vital to bond with your baby, bump, birth and beyond.

She needed to make oxytocin. Then would come love: Not the kind of love she'd resisted – the nebulous, sentimental, unreliable kind. Not the love located theatrically in your heart, but the molecular, definite, structural kind. Love as a logical, provable formula: $C_{43}H_{66}N_{12}O_{12}S_2$.

I will $C_{43}H_{66}N_{12}O_{12}S_2$ you. And then I'll get to know you, and we can take it from there.

She returned to her folder and made a new section: How To Create Oxytocin.

> *Sing to your baby. Choose a song and repeat it. When your baby is born, it will remember this song and it will bring them comfort and calm.*

She tried a different song in the shower every morning. How do you decide an anthem for a land that does not yet exist?

> *Talk to your baby. Connect physically through your bump. Touch is crucial for stimulating oxytocin before birth.*

What was she touching? A foot? An elbow? These fleeting angles jutting out her flesh.

Once, when she'd lived in South Africa, she'd gone out in a boat to find whales. A glimpse, fragmented, then gone again, piercing the surface, disappearing, a tease.

The mystery of the whales had been thrilling. The mystery of her own flesh was not.

This is how you changed me, my firstborn: you showed me that mystery is an act of trust.

Oxytocin comes from the Greek for 'quick birth'. She tried to flood the baby with it, doing everything the book said. But it wasn't enough. It took forty hours to break her. Not enough oxytocin. No quick birth. A home birth – she was adamant, no hospitals. Forty hours of refusing to get naked, not letting anyone touch her, or even talk. Stubborn and controlling, everything clenched shut.

A day passed, a night passed, another day. Her gran had to buy two newspapers, anticipating the marking of her first great-grand-child's birth.

She was stubborn, she was scared, and she was failing. How was it possible? She'd had a six-page plan.

She knew what she was meant to do. She'd prepared for months. Spent every night listening to the hypnobirthing CD. She was meant to let go, to visualise rainbows, to breathe. *Breathe in love . . . breathe out pain. Each contraction takes you closer to your baby.*

Each contraction was an advance of an enemy. Her body, a castle. Drawbridge up, portcullis down.

It took forty hours to blast the castle open, and because of her blockading, the baby was born near dead.

At the last minute, she'd gripped tighter.

No – she wouldn't push, couldn't push. No.

She trapped it. It got stuck inside her.

She wouldn't push. Wouldn't. No. No.

It took its first breath inside her and suffocated.

The midwife reached in and yanked it out like a calf.

They snatched him away – a him now – to the nursery, with the rocking chair and bunting and animals on the walls.

The midwife was counting. They were trying to resuscitate.

He's grey, he's grey, her mother had said.

An ambulance sirened. No cry from the nursery.

Her first words as a mother were: *What have I done.*

It took three and a half minutes for her firstborn to live. The Mother stood naked, drenched in blood, shit, sweat. This wasn't a birth. It was a crime scene. *I killed my baby. I was never meant to be a mum.* Three and a half minutes. *I killed my baby.*

If you tell yourself something enough times, it becomes true.

At the hospital, they told her she was lucky. Didn't even need stitches, and the baby was fine. More than fine – healthy, strong and bonny.

You'll be happy to hear we're sending you home!

Happy? She was not happy. Home was a crime scene. Everything was wrong. She was not meant to be a mother. Her baby always knew it. He did not want to be her son.

He cried and cried.
> She had broken his heart.

He never, ever slept.
> She'd made him scared of the dark.

He was active, with a fierceness.
> She'd made him want to escape.

He wouldn't latch on.
> She couldn't keep him alive.

Oxytocin stimulates milk production. That same oxytocin is then passed on through the breast. The book had said: *Feeding your baby builds attachment. You are literally feeding them your love.*

But she was broken. She'd always known she was broken.

I cannot be a mother. I am incapable of love.

She was a bad mum who couldn't even feed her baby. She tried and tried. He kept losing weight. If anyone dared formula, she raged at them. She had to feed him herself. Else there'd never be love.

All the books, the lactation mentors, the drop-ins and advice groups didn't help.

Any chance he's tongue-tied? her oldest friend asked.

What's tongue-tied? Nobody mentioned it. Nobody checked. Was I supposed to check? It wasn't in the books.

The baby *was* tongue-tied. It was too late to fix it. But he was clever. He found his own way. He started feeding, and the feeding got easier, and he grew so plump and strong.

This is what you taught me, my firstborn: put down the books and I'll show you the way.

Water helped put them back together. Maybe they weren't destined to meet on land.

It started with baths. He was so happy in the water. They waited weeks to bathe him, like the book had said. Weeks of him crying, no stillness. The minute his skin felt water, he was calm.

A baby tub at first. Then she ran a bath and got in with him. He lay on her palms, swirling on the surface, a soft-breeze lily in a sacred pond. She anointed his head with her fingertips. The first time he fed properly was in the bath.

The Mother took him swimming, in a specialist baby pool. Silent and warm, lights low. A holy place to baptise their union. Finally, the Mother let go. Of herself, of her baby. Of his body. The teacher said he was ready. Let go.

He'll swim to you, she said. Trust your baby.

And just like that, he swam underwater. A mer-babe, a selkie, a fish. His huge eyes open, finding hers, underwater. He swam into her arms, and she held him so close.

From that day on, they always sought water. A bath, a river, a pool. She'd lift him, water-kissed, and swaddle him close to her. She saw it was true, what everyone said – he was beautiful. Big squashy mouth, huge dark eyes, olive skin. The way the water jewelled his long eyelashes. The stillness, in both of them, when they sat like this. The wonder, the silence, the healing, the peace.

How much do our birth stories shape us? If the Mother had let her son arrive with ease into the world, would he still have been as independent, as determined, as bold? He was always so busy. Took all milestones seriously, smashing them way ahead of time.

Sometimes, she thinks those last dangerous seconds inside her left him with a mantra: *I'll do it myself.*

This baby of hers, this miracle of a baby, grew into a remarkable child. Three and he could already read. Memorised entire books off by heart. Four, he beat adults at chess. Got into MENSA with full marks aged ten.

The first time he told her he loved her, he wrote it in Morse code. She framed the scrap of paper. The dots meant more than he could know.

And tomorrow, he will turn thirteen. She doesn't know how they did it. But they did it, somehow. It was nothing like her folder or textbooks. What little solace came from the science of her cells. They learnt the unteachable through, and with, and from, each other: love and relinquishment, dependency, faith.

This is what you taught me, my firstborn: that there are many types of knowledge and so many kinds of love.

She wraps his present, a proper telescope, while he's sleeping. She decorates the house with bunting and balloons. She thinks, as she sometimes does, about that Other Life. The one in which she's adamant about never having kids.

In that Other Life, she lives in Berlin, or Paris. A generous aunt, spontaneous godmother, babysitting friend. Lovers of both genders, that she never commits to. No children, but a gentle Great Dane, like Toby-Dog, that she names Golitha after her favourite spot on Bodmin Moor.

What is her body, in this Other Life? Does she continue to act like she doesn't have one at all? Does she ever make peace with the language of her body? Does she carry on hurting it, taming it, fighting it, starving it of food, sleep, nourishment, love?

At what point does she accept a tender contract with her body to nurture it, in return for keeping her alive?

Maybe she doesn't. She dies young, in this Other Life. Suicide was always a card in her back pocket after all.

Her firstborn, too, likes to philosophise other existences. A branch of science that has always fascinated him, drawn him in. When he was seven – he'd read Steven Hawking and understood it – he said:

I bet you can't be in a thousand places at once! I CAN.

The Mother expected him to sprint to a range of locations. Instead, he closed his eyes and stood very still. A minute or so passed, then he began giggling, huge eyes euphoric.

See Mummy! I can be everywhere and everything! All at the same time! It's called Infinite Possibility Theory and it's quantum mechanics. You try!

This is what you taught me, my firstborn: you can be anyone and everyone. Just believe, and close your eyes.

He wakes up, thirteen. How did they get here. Beautifully, extraordinarily, impossibly, thirteen.

Thirteen, and my god, I love you, with a beautiful, extraordinary, impossible force.

He opens his birthday card. It's a diagram of oxytocin. He reads the Mother's looping handwriting inside:

> *Seventy years ago, in 1953, a scientist called Vincent du Vigneaud discovered the meaning of love — a peptide molecule consisting of nine amino acids with a molecular mass of 1007 Daltons. He was the first to identify, analyse and synthesise oxytocin, winning the Nobel Prize for, essentially, recreating love.*

Thirteen years ago, I discovered the meaning of love — and I've been rediscovering it every day of our 4,745 days together since. It is more than nine amino acids and 1007 Daltons. It is letting go, listening, and learning. It is a living kind of love, one that changes, flows, unfixed. There are no words for it, no numbers, no formulae. It is a knowingness beyond anything we can know.

> *You have shown me that. You changed me, my firstborn. Your birth was my birth too.*

She ends the card with:

> *I $C_{43}H_{66}N_{12}O_{12}S_2$ you.*

He smiles as he deciphers it. The Mother smiles too.

I'm never having children. She'd always said that. A child breaks you open, shattering the pieces that make you *you*. Motherhood, she thought, would raid the cabinet of her is-ness. Better keep it locked, keep her artefacts safe and secret, unshared.

This is what you taught me, my firstborn: that my pieces are your pieces, just as your pieces are mine. That love is tumbling everything out that cabinet and revelling in them, rolling in them, tossing them hand to hand. That when we do that, when we all tip our cabinets wide open, for everyone, we can create and curate a museum all of our own. A museum of memories, stories, knowledge, more vivid, more meaningful, than a lonely cabinet, gathering dust, in a cold dark room.

The Huer's Wife

What are you writing about, Mum? asks the eldest.

About you actually, the Mother says. When you were born.

Will you write about when I was born, asks the younger one. I was an easy baby, wasn't I. I was a nicer baby than him.

You were the second, she says. Second's always easier.

Well you should definitely put my birth story in the book, it's really good.

Very well, she says.

And so she begins.

Once upon a time, a boy was born with magic and folklore already in his bones.

A second child, his mother didn't need a folder. Her firstborn had written all the books she could need. She had recalibrated Perfect to Good Enough. She trusted her body now. Her firstborn gifted that to her.

It was like in South Africa, when she had looked for whales a second time. Now she knew what to look for, shapes emerged from the ocean's cloth. Whole long bodies in all their magnificence, surfacing in fragments, swimming under the boat. Marvel replaced uncertainty, as it did with this pregnancy. He was a person already to her. He had a name.

And so the baby grew inside that trust and knowingness, and when it was time, he was excited to be born, as if he had spent those months getting ready for a party that he couldn't wait to get to, that wouldn't start till he'd arrived.

No forty-hour labour. It was forty minutes. The Mother went into the kitchen for a glass of water at dinnertime and came out with a newborn, sleepily snuggling in her arms.

Her toddler, her mum, her auntie-mum and uncle were there with her. The boy's Father almost was not. He was at work. Only half an hour away. Her waters hadn't broken yet. Plenty of time, they said.

I don't think so, she replied.

So the Father rushed home and immediately knew that it was imminent. He had helped deliver their first child. But with a midwife not able to come to them at such short notice, he'd be delivering this one by himself.

Her uncle, busy trying to inflate the birth pool, came into the kitchen to connect the hose.

I don't think there's time for that, said the Father.

Her auntie-mum took the toddler to read upstairs. She had to read very loudly, to cover up the sounds from the Mother below.

The Mother didn't make that much noise though. Instead, she leaned on the counter and breathed. She opened herself up and surrendered to it, letting go so easily compared with the first time. Actually she was smiling, smiling and half laughing, because it was hilarious and ridiculous and exhilarating fun.

The hospital, unable to send a midwife, told her mum to dial 999. The landline cord only stretched to the doorway of the kitchen, so her mum had to relay information to the Father, crouched on the floor, beneath the Mother, who was still leaning on the kitchen counter, by the grimacing pumpkins they'd just carved for Hallowe'en.

The Mother was pushing. Letting her instincts take over.

I can see the head! cried the Father.

He can see the head, her mum said to the phone.

Wait, the Father said – it's not a head! It's not a head!

It's not a head, her mum said, calmly but alarmed.

Like a head but not a head! Like an alien!

Like a head but not a head, her mum calmly told the phone.

The boys both giggle as she reenacts the story, even though they've heard it a million times. For the youngest, it confirms he is special. For the eldest, it confirms his brother was an alien after all. She's laughing too, as she tells it. It's joyous and brilliant. One of the best moments of her life.

No, her waters haven't broken yet, her mum was telling the telephone.

Then abruptly –

> Okay, she orders, okay – stop pushing – they said you
> have to let him slide out.

The Mother stopped pushing. Everything quiet. Suspended.

Then the Father started laughing, that breathless laugh where belief meets disbelief. A wet white sack slid out of the woman into his hands. He held it carefully.

The baby was inside.

The telephone said he mustn't pop it. Just let the baby find its own way out into the world.

And so, once upon a time, a baby was born, a very special birth, because he was born in the caul.

> And that's why I'll never drown, he declares, ten years
> later.

> You'll never drown because you'll be careful, the
> Mother corrects him. But yes. That's how the old
> story goes.

Isn't that where all old stories come from? The inexplicable, the unexpected, the rare. Birth. Death. Love. Shipwrecks. Eclipses. Things that are out of the ordinary scare us. We need words to catch them and keep us safe. Control. That's all language is. Control. Sense out of non-sense. Meaning from mystery. Patterns in randomness. Hope in the dark. Call it religion, mythology, mysticism. Call it literature. Call it fate.

That's why children need stories. So little of their world makes sense. So much unknowable, unshowable. Unnameable. Retelling his birth lets him clutch hold of a thread.

He wasn't just any baby – he was a Caulbearer.

Caulbearers are destined for greatness.

Caulbearers cannot drown.

Caulbearers can predict weather and harvests. They can divine water when it's deep underground.

Lawyers carried cauls to win court cases. Sailors bought cauls to protect them from the sea. Miners kept cauls to keep away explosions.

Many languages have caulish idioms to describe someone born lucky – *born in a bonnet* they say in Poland, *born with a hat on* goes the French.

The boy is a quarter French, an eighth Polish. His ancestors somewhere are nodding with pride.

The woman likes to imagine herself giving birth like this two hundred years ago, in a fisherman's cottage by the sea. She is a huer's wife, in this story, in her hometown in Cornwall, an important port back then.

The huer had a special job in those boom years of fishing. The Sea-Watcher. Shoal-Seeker. The Beckoner. The Guide. The man who waited all day on the flat stone roof of the white clifftop huer's hut, looking out over the vast blue bay.

In the story, she is proud to be the huer's wife. Huers had a very special gift – to spot the moon in the middle of the day. Not the sky-moon. The fish-moon: the silvery crescent the shoals of pilchards on the surface made.

Six months of the year her husband was at the huer's hut, every day, all weather, no matter what, watching over the entire stretch of sea. Sitting there patiently smoking his pipe, all beard and big broad mouth and navy overalls, and a book – because in this story, they are still a bookish family – or maybe a sketchpad that he hides from the other men. Sitting there, with his long brass trumpet, and bunches of dry furze for the signal, ready to light. The boats all out in the harbour, waiting for his call. Like all huers, her husband knows his 'stem', his patch and its behaviours, reading the movements of the water's surface like she could read thoughts on her firstborn's face.

She is the huer's wife, and she is proud of it. One day, her first-born son will be the next huer too. Huers learn the art from their fathers, who learnt it from their fathers and their fathers before that. Sometimes her husband takes their firstborn up with

147

him, taking his place in the dip in that roof, worn by all the men who had sat watching there before.

How nice, to have no choice, she thinks. To be born into a role. To see moons in the day. Instead of being stuck in the house, cooking and cleaning, a toddler tugging on your apron and another due any day.

Hours go past of nothing. Increasingly, this season, they can wait days and days. Widow Tregorran gossiped the huer wasn't fit for it, that's why it's been a bad spell, and some liked to believe her – because what if the truth of it, what if the actual fact of the matter was, the sea just held less and less fish.

Her husband got upset by their whispers. Upset by the stares of the wageless fishermen at the quay. He prayed hard each night, they both did. But a week went by, and still no catch.

> Today will be the day, he'd said that morning. Get your cake-making ready!

He rubbed her belly for luck.

And it was the day. All morning she listened for it – the sound of his trumpet signalling the call. She heard his shouts, heard the crackle of the furze lighting, and the baby moved inside her with an almighty force.

> Hevva! Hevva! his big voice is crying, which means
> *They are here! They are here!*

And he's up on his feet, waving his arms in patterns to direct the fishermen to the catch.

Right off! he shouts.

Win tow!

Cowl rooze! Cowl rooze!

And off they go, the seiners and riggers, casting out their giant nets. The huer's wife knows these nets well, she has been repairing them with her needles since she was a girl. Enormous, huge rectangles of woven mesh, weighted with lead to sink the trap to the ocean floor.

Out these huge nets come, shooting from the side of the two biggest boats, the noise thundering round the bay like the sea rising in applause.

Then the smaller boats, the sheepdogs, come herding, casting a smaller net around the shoal, closing in on the flip-flopping huddle, tightening their grip for the kill, seagulls and guillemots divebombing, gannets and cormorants swooping into the fray, and the town erupting, all the women and children running, out their higgledy-piggledy cottages and down the cobbled lanes to the quay.

The huer's wife hears the commotion but she doesn't go running. She is about to give birth.
She is about to give birth, earlier than due. Every heave from the fishermen to pull the pilchards is a heave of her stomach, the tightening of the net, and her husband is there, and the cake isn't ready, and she calms herself and stirs the raisins into

the batter, the lines of the old rhyme rhythming her mind – *The Pilchards are come, and heva is heard / And the town from the top to the bottom is stirred* –

Her neighbours' doors slamming all around her, the clip-clop of clogs, and whoops running to the port – *The Pilchards are come, and heva is heard* – shawls flying past her window to the harbour, her firstborn hurling himself down the stairs –

Can I go, can I go?

Go on with you, find Netty next door.

– and so her little son joins them all running, *The town from the top to the bottom is stirred*, joining the town on the jetty as the men dump load after load on the quay, the women in pairs rolling out huge barrels, the old boys opening the salt cellar huts, and the children shovelling all the salt they can into buckets and pouring it over the writhing fish.

The huer's wife breathes. Her husband will be home soon, after he's taken his knife and notched a catch mark in the roof. He'll come home and the hevva cake won't be ready, or worse, it will have burnt – she can smell it now, in the oven – the waves going through her, as she clutches the counter, leans her head in the mess of lard, flour, currants, sugar, cream – and her husband rushes in –

Wife! Do you have the cake for me?

Wife? But – Wife! What's going on?

Take the cake out, 'tis burning!

Is it the babe?

The cake, Husband!

So he takes out the cake, which sits there simmering, and says he'll go get Netty, she'll know what to do.

Netty's not there! You'll have to—

He looks flustered. It is highly irregular, but they have no choice.

So he kneels on the floor. Lifts his standing wife's skirts up. Gently pulls down her drawers, his fingers slipping in the blood and the stickiness, but it was like lambing, it was natural, he didn't mind.

It wasn't just natural – it was beautiful. Miraculous, joyful, his wife so calm – the warmth beneath the skirts of her quickening body, the afternoon sunlight painting the kitchen gold, the smell of cinnamon and raisin and sugar, and yes – now the head, his child's head, begins to emerge – and as he reaches up his hands, he feels a rush of God.

Why can't all fathers experience this? If they did, they'd go more willingly to church.

How different this was from her first birth. How long and awful that had been. How Netty had breathed life into that still grey body, like she'd saved him from drowning in a wreck.

God passes through his hands into his baby, as it slips out easily into the huer's waiting palms.

Well I never, Wife.

She looks down at her husband. At the white sack in his hands. She kneels beside him, her hands beside his hands, the callouses on his and the flour on hers. The white sack wriggling and moving for a moment. Then a hand breaking through. Then a foot. Then a head.

A caul-bearer . . . breathes the huer.

A caul-bearer baby. The first in the village. A miracle, a gift.

Tell the rest of the story, Mum, nags the youngest. Because then loads of people came . . .

Yes, says the Mother. There were twelve of us!

Was I there? asks the eldest.

Of course! By then you were in bed.

And then cheese on toast! says the youngest.

Yes, she says. And then cheese on toast for twelve.

She laughs, shakes her head at the absurdity. He was born minutes before the ambulance arrived. The paramedic marched in, expecting an emergency. He turned all the lights on. The Father turned them off.

Thank god, the paramedic said when he saw them.
Have to admit, I haven't done a birth before.

He knelt down, did some checks, got the scissors, poised to cut not the baby's end, but the Mother's end, of the umbilical cord.

Maybe a bit closer to his actual bellybutton? said the Father.

Right, yes. You do the honours, the paramedic said.

The Father cut the cord. The baby looked up at them. They wrapped him in blankets and she brought him to her breast.

For some reason, a mix-up maybe, another ambulance arrived, then shortly after that the midwife too. But there wasn't much to do, so they all sat there, in the living room, her mum and uncle and auntie-mum and two teams of paramedics and the midwife and the Mother and the Father and new baby, who immediately latched on and fed quietly.

And then I got up and made everyone cheese on toast! the Mother says.

She can't remember, but of course the placenta must have birthed out too.

But you didn't keep the caul did you, says the eldest. Because that would be really weird.

Of course, in the other story, the huer's wife keeps it. Hangs it up carefully to dry above the stove, with a garland of rosemary and lavender to cure it. Everyone comes to see it, to touch. Some of the fishermen and miners ask for a price.

The huer's wife laughs. Of course, they'll never sell it. They'll never let go of this luck.

After his birth, the catches are plentiful, almost every day for the two weeks of fishing left. At season's end, the huer and his wife stroll to the quayside, their two-week-old in her arms. They couldn't miss the troyl. She'd made stargazy pie.

Their firstborn runs ahead of them to the net lofts where the cèilidh band's music pours out – fiddles and bodhráns and accordions, dancing feet stamping in time to old songs, three three-hand reels and lattapuch steps that make you glad the net loft beams are so strong, the dancers skidding on slopped-out cider, and on all of them, gloriously, the silver stink of fish.

It was the last troyl in that quay town. Her husband the last huer. There were no more fish.

When the tin had gone, too many turned to pilchards. And the pilchards weren't an infinite blessing after all. The town became destitute. The young all left – to seek their fortunes in new mines in South Africa and Australia, or to faraway cities when factories called.

The huer's family stayed. He still sits on the huer's hut. He sketches the sea. His eldest boy draws too. The huer's wife takes in sewing from Lady Wortley at the Big House. When they have special occasions up there, she cooks for them and cleans. Her youngest, the caul-bearer, goes swimming. At least she doesn't have to worry he'll drown.

But times get harder. They take the caul out its special chest. The huer's wife sells it to Lord Wortley, who is charmed. It hangs in the Great Hall, and she hears him boasting about it to distinguished visitors as she's serving them silver spoons of tiny peas.

Her son doesn't drown, but he follows his brother to Cape Town. They work in a mine. She never meets their wives.

There's a new song now. She sings it, quietly, as her bones creak, mopping the Big House floor.

> *Cornish lads are fishermen*
> *and Cornish lads are miners too.*
> *But when the fish and tin are gone,*
> *what are Cornish boys to do?*

No songs for Cornish girls though. What's a Cornish girl to do?

The Mother gives her second-born a Cornish name. A name she had wanted for him since he was conceived. It means happiness, and from birth it seemed made for him. She always thought she'd raise her children in Cornwall. Now she has to raise Cornwall in them. Or maybe, if they'll be Sussex children, she'll have to give them old Sussex words and knowledge instead.

She wishes she had kept the caul now. Dried it with rosemary and wrapped it carefully in a chest. To take it out sometimes and draw magic from it. When life tosses her like a shipwreck and she fears she might drown.

Water Plus Seed Plus Light

This house? Are you sure?

She nodded.

We'll have to gut it. You won't be able to move in for
a while.

The tenant had just died, after living his whole life here, in this
tucked-away cottage on the lane up to the Downs. The Aga was
dead. Upstairs stank of dog piss. Binbags filled the halls.

That's fine. I'll wait.

A house is a house. It was the garden she wanted. The wildness,
the hermitude. The breath. Never mind what the landlords saw:
three smashed greenhouses, nettles taller than her children,
briars thicker than your arm. Asbestos pipes hanging off the
outhouse. A clapped-out car spilling its guts over the grass.
Barbed wire tongues lolling out of rotten fences, and cat shit all
over the path.

She saw her own wounds in the wounds of this garden and knew
they could bring each other back to life.

★ ★ ★ ★

Bennet knew everyone and everyone knew Bennet. He was born in the village to parents born here before him. A lad when he followed his dad into a job at the Big House, gardening for the lord and lady who owned every brick and acre for miles around. Bennet was a natural gardener, in charge of the greenhouses, magicking the veg.

He'd stay in that job all his life, and barely leave the village as there wasn't any need. Nice cottage on the winding sheeptrack, with a front and back garden he made beautiful from scratch. Little school for his children, village shop, church, cricket club, and a cosy old pub for one or two after work. He had a bike with a bell to cycle round the village, popping the weekly news-letter through each door. In winter, he wore his wife-knitted bobble hat that made everybody smile.

Time passed comfortably, as it does in small villages, the church bells marking hours, and funerals the years, and Bennet — with his bicycle and bobble hat, with his prize-winning tomatoes by an honesty box outside, with his cross-eyed collie that once drank a whole pint in the pub, and the children who still lived down the road and came home for Sunday roasts — Bennet grew into the warm eccentricity expected, or earned, in such a place.

He was born here, belonged here, and would die here. Nothing could make a man much happier than that.

★ ★ ★ ★

The house was gutted and made good enough. The woman and her children moved there in spring. Buds peeping out the clod again, sensing it was safe to come out. The garden had been violated – gutted, burnt and bulldozed. Bonfires for weeks, the neighbours said. And what a bloody palaver, dragging out that old car.

The boys whooped off, finding sticks and climbing trees. They saw adventure. She saw paradise. Everyone else saw a lot of hard work.

How do you measure an acre? They didn't know, but guessed it might be half. She walked the sad fenceless perimeter of earth that circled the house. She wouldn't rush into anything in this garden. All that mattered was to listen to it. Earn back its trust. Light plus water plus seed, the age-old formula for life, for hope.

She was gentle with the ground she'd been given. Tilled, trowelled and tended. Not forcing it to her will. Each month brought astonishment. Everything braving up from below. She noticed that, once, it must have been beautiful. That the tenant before her had made magic here. Known what he was doing. Roses, flowerbeds, paths, just so.

Every day, it offered up new secrets. A courtyard discovered. A Japanese quince. There was so much left of his life in the earth here. Buried toys, rusty tools, weathered gnomes with no heads.

How thriving it must have been once. But what a ruin when she'd moved in. In between, there must be a story. And if you don't know the facts, you make it up.

How much easier it is to imagine men than know them. Dead men are easiest. You can make them so nice.

★ ★ ★ ★

Bennet wasn't a man to let things trouble him, but when he felt some sort of damp creep in, he'd go to the long Victorian glasshouse sheltered between espaliered fruit trees against the Big House boundary wall. It was quiet and warm, and he could be alone there, the scent of it so comforting, the faith of seeing things grow. Cucumbers and tomatoes, floor to ceiling. Earth mixed with hop dregs and the stable's manure. Even after he'd retired, he'd still seek out its refuge. Pilfer vegetables for the trug. Lob snails out the door. Nice chat with one of the lads he'd trained, in their thirties now, but he still thought of them as boys.

Once he went to the glasshouse and discovered he was not alone. A man sat painting at one end. Bennet kept himself to himself at the other, until he grew suspicious the artist was painting him too. More and more of this type in the village. They called themselves bohemians. The village called them layabouts. No soil or scars on their hands.

In that moment, he missed the other glasshouses. This was the only one left. There'd been seven, when he was a boy, and a mushroom house too that was musty and dark, and one for strawberries that ripened on roof shelves with a pulley you brought down slowly till they were low enough to pick. Lost to the war. He was five when they fell. Night, and he ran into his mother's bed. The boom of the bomb, the crash and whirr, and the smashing that came in waves as all the windows in the village shook out. The doodlebug took every glasshouse but this one.

Hope – that was what it stood for. The resilience of fragile things.

★ ★ ★ ★

The woman and the garden grew into each other. She planted flowers, vegetables, trees. She dug a pond with her hands by moonlight. Built fences, archways, made new paths. Hung bird-feeders, got chickens, set up beehives. She'd needed hope, and bit by bit, she was finding it. Water plus seed plus light.

The boys wove their own threads of belonging – a water-fight hideout, a swing on a branch, the start of a treehouse, an insect zoo. Dragonfly exoskeletons collected from the pond, and bones and pottery shards from deep underground. A sparrow's nest, abandoned, that they preserved in the freezer, then sprayed with resin to hang on the wall.

In the summer, they camped in the garden. Their home was home to extraordinary skies. Pitch black, silent, star-full. Bats skittering round overhead. Three planets visible over the back fence – Saturn, Jupiter and Mars – and Venus out the front, in the evening. Their little hands clutching telescopes, lying out on blankets, ears pricked for the hedgehogs that rustled through the gaps in the hedge. They learnt the old Sussex term for them, *prickleback urchins*, and *mousearknicles* for dragonflies, *flittermouse* for bat.

Gift after gift from this garden. Such abundance. Nothing wasted. Each season, a feast.

September brought so many apples – six, seven hundred – that picking and cooking and storing them became a full-time job.

October, and crates full of walnuts, drying for Christmas in the outhouse, that took her back to another life in France – young, in the middle of nowhere, with her half-French former partner, before they had their sons.

In this other life – cooking soup by candlelight, power cut after power cut, storm after storm, drinking the neighbour's wine, running through sunflowers, swimming in rivers, picking peaches juicy and warm, driving tractors, happy, alone, trawling jumble sales, watching fireworks at fêtes – in this other life, when they were young and creating a life together, they'd spent months harvesting walnuts and lugging them to markets to sell. So she knew three types of walnut, and how to lay them out on the floor and turn them with a broom carefully each day to dry, how to tell when they're ready, and make dye from the skins.

Living. That was what this was now. Maybe for the first time in her life. Living – in the land, in each other, in their skins, in the present. They rarely left. No need. They had this cottage, this garden, the school. The shop and the post office. New friends.

And she had the Gardener – for this is what she called him – the man who left this garden, who she talked to in her mind. He spoke to her through bulbs and trowel-clinks. She asked him questions and he offered up replies.

She liked him showing her what to do. She hadn't had a male voice in her head for a long time.

> Here, girl – see this line of daffodils? Well that marks where I put my path.

That's a much better place than my path. Shall we move it back?

She found a rampant honeysuckle, smothered by briars and bindweed. Her shears kept hitting something hard.

What's this?

Keep going, girl.

A post. Buckled metal. Wooden ribs.

You had an arbour here.

That's right, girl.

She had already put a bench there before finding it. The spot had the best sunset view.

She found tiny cars, a head of an Action Man, a little red spade, a dismembered doll.

My grandchildren, he laughed.

She turned his workshop into a studio, his workbench her writing desk. Everything she found – rusty tools, rope coils, oil lamps – she hung on the wall to display.

Why did you leave all this stuff, she asked him.

Didn't leave it, girl. The earth took it. It'll take your
stuff too.

★ ★ ★ ★

Bennet wasn't a man who kept stuff. His wife was, mind. Thought
everything had a use. An unspoken agreement, at some point in
their marriage, that he would have the garden, and she would
have the house. He kept his kingdom tidy. Everything just so.

The car, then, came as a surprise to everyone. He took down
the fence, and his mechanic friend towed it from the field. Parked
it right there, on his nice neat lawn, between the apple trees
and greenhouse. He didn't have a licence. He'd never learnt to
drive.

But his son, see, he was into cars, and Bennet thought – now
he'd retired – well, they could regain lost time together, doing
it up. Because maybe his wife was right, he hadn't done enough
with the children. Didn't know them like she did. That's why
it was awkward, these tensions, these distances, that seemed to
fall over them during Sunday roasts.

To be fair, his son tried, and Bennet tried. But it wasn't like
he'd imagined it in his head, and eventually his son made excuses,
didn't have enough time to tinker with old engines. He had his
work, he had his kids.

Still, Bennet kept the car in the garden. Lifted the bonnet now
and then. Got a manual and took it apart. Then he did his back
in, the car's innards left scattered all over the grass. Jim from
the garage offered to buy it, but Bennet held on.

164

The bad back put an end to his gardening. That, and the death of his wife. Weeds grew. Brambles took over. The clematis on the outhouse brought the tiles off the roof. Nettles strangled the veg beds. Walnuts gone to squirrels. Apples gone to rot.

Time passed. The village was changing. He knew fewer people and fewer people knew him. Families wanted towns now. Pub prices went up, the number of regulars went down. The vicar changed. The lord remarried. Then his neighbour Bob moved out. A good old boy, they'd brewed cider from windfalls. They'd known each other since school. Both called Robert – that's why Bennet was known by his surname. Always one wife round the others', baking and blathering. But Mabel died and Bob gave it up. Too big, he said, I'm just rattling around.

Bennet knew he'd never give up like that. If he could, he'd be buried in this ground.

★ ★ ★ ★

They hadn't been there long when she first became ill. Lyme disease, dismissed by doctors till her body shut down, tick-bite toxin permeating her blood, brain, bones. Hospitals and ambulances. Pain. Fevers. Arthritis. Fingers that wouldn't unclaw from her hand. Then seizures. Memory loss. Scans.

We've found something in your brain.

That tick was a blessing. How else would they have known.

Her body held secrets she didn't want to think about. Her garden held secrets it revealed every day.

165

For two months, no one could tell her if her time was up. The garden became even more vital to her than before. A place to plant herself into, like the Gardener. To leave fragments of herself behind. She bought two white mulberry saplings. Be years before they fruit, someone frowned. She didn't mind. The fruit was for her children. To taste something of their shared sweetness on their tongues when she was gone.

Her mum moved in for a while, to help with the boys, and the garden became her garden too. She wore a wide-brimmed hat and blue overalls, and dug with the same purpose her daughter recognised in herself. Her mum bought a polytunnel and cleared a space to put it up. Cucumbers, salad, tomatoes grew prolific and quick. The chickens made magic compost that her mother called black gold.

It was crushing, then, just crushing, devastating, that first tornado of wind. How it swept down from the hills so violently, and tore through the garden with such force. Polytunnel stripped to metal carcass. The panes of the greenhouse obliterated, broken beams swaying and then collapsing in the mud. And her passion-flower archway – the last gift from her grandmother – buckled and boned on the path.

Is this the story? she asked the Gardener. Is this how the ruin set in?

★ ★ ★ ★

It was a place where the day was told through weather. The strength and direction of the wind. Such wind; newcomers couldn't stomach it. Huge gales, blustering up from the sea and

166

gaining speed as they rushed over the Downs. East to west, there was nothing to stop it, the house the tallest thing in its path.

Bennet paid no mind. He'd grown up with it. He knew what to plant and what wouldn't stand a chance. Knew not to get too attached to anything. The storms of '87 brought down two sycamores, one just avoiding the house, and the Douglas fir between him and his neighbour blocked the road till the tractor dragged it out.

Still, he persisted with his greenhouses. How else would he get those tomatoes everyone liked. And he enjoyed it, this tug of war between him and the elements. Each storm a sermon – a lesson in acceptance, and afterwards, an opportunity to heal and forgive.

He respected the winds. It was humbling. They'd been here long before him and they'd go on after he was gone. He was just a temporary guardian of this land. And it was satisfying, the post-storm repair. Gathering the glass, replacing the panes. Stripping back the sealant and taping it back again. He knew to grow his veg down the middle, not the sides.

Still, he would stay up all night when it was howling, just as his mother had done when he was a boy. She'd loved this garden and felt the pain of its assault, and he felt her pain and liked to keep her company as she watched.

So the *yesty* storms brought her back to him, blowing her language back into his mind. She was dead, but she was next to him at the window, as they watched the *swallocky* clouds gather, listening to the wind *belver* down the *bostal* to engulf the garden in *whiffles*

167

that shuddered your bones, the driving *scud* beating on the window, as the smash began outside.

He'd stay awake, as she had done, to keep vigil till the gods had done their work.

But unlike his mother, who'd be devastated the next morning when she went down to survey the wreck – treelings sidewards, flower beds sodden and veg patches *swarved*, *rhythes* of water flooding paths – unlike his mother, who felt the loss so keenly, he'd just shake his head, look heavenwards and laugh.

But then it was always his job to make her feel better. Something he never seemed to achieve.

★ ★ ★ ★

The woman was devastated when those first storms hit. Overwhelmed by the havoc and loss. Feeling responsible – the garden had trusted her. She'd let this garden, and the Gardener, down. This land was her body. She'd wrecked her body too.

Slowly, she set about rebuilding. Just got things better, when another storm came. Then another. Then another. So this was winter here, this will always be winter. What three seasons gave, one season took away.

She understood it now, the original ruin – smashed glass two feet mudward, the bits and pieces buried underground. She understood the schema for his planting. The things that survived of him here were sheltered from the winds. She stopped begrudging the elements and fell into their rhythms. Nine months abundance, three months loss.

She learnt to accept it. To see it as a dance. Repaired the polytunnel and moved it somewhere more sheltered. Rebuilt the fences. Poured concrete round posts. Built a fence out of skip-scavenged panels to divide the front and back, to act as a buffer between the lime trees and lilacs. Taped up the greenhouse and screwed in batons to reinforce it. Planted things that stayed low to the ground.

Began again. Then again. Then again.

Did the same with her body, which got stronger through it all.

The thing that still bothered her though was the mud. The garden, like everything here, was on the squiff. The ground tilted and slid into the centre like an under-baked cake. Not noticeable in the summer – but then the rain, rain, rain. How it ran down the slant and formed a river, fast-flowing, flooding the path.

The mud. She'd never known mud like it. Ankle-deep, thick and clingy. The dog and the children traipsed it all over the house. Everything had mud on. The only thing she couldn't fix.

★ ★ ★ ★

Mud. Now his mother had words in her Sussex dialect for that. Him and some of the old boys tried to list them in the pub. There was a barmaid, new to the village, and she couldn't tell when they were serious and when they were pulling her leg. They got to twenty-five words then stopped counting:

Cledgy – mud that stuck to your spade.

Gawm – stinky, sticky mud.

Gubber – black rotting compost.

You're making these up now, the barmaid said.

But they kept on. *Sleech* – silty river mud. *Stug* was watery. *Swank* was a bog. The thickest of all called *slub*.

And when we walk in here with our muddy boots on,
Bennet told her. You can tell us to stop *stabbling* before
we make your nice floor all *slommaky*.

All those words his mother had for mud, but none to tell him she was proud of him, after all.

★ ★ ★ ★

Pallets. That would do it. She scavenged and scrounged as many as she could. Lifted up all the *sleechy*, *slubby* paving and levelled a long row of pallets from the back door to the gate. When she put all the slabs on top of them, the path rose above the ground, half a foot high.

She called it the Boardwalk.

Catwalk! squealed her youngest, promptly strutting
with his chest out, waving to an imaginary audience,
posing, head high down the path.

Three years they'd been here. Hard, hard years. Life had given them a lot of *gawmy slub*. The village was changing. Rents going up. She always owed a month, sometimes two months, three. Every day she panicked her home would be taken from her. How could she leave? She had poured herself into this garden. She started planting pots, moveable, ownable, instead.

★ ★ ★ ★

In those last years, Bennet hardly went into the garden. Spent more and more time in bed, propped on his pillows, old collie at his feet. The garden he enjoyed was outside his window now – the tops of the magnolia, the elderflowers, lilacs, the huge old walnut tree by the road.

As a boy he had climbed up that walnut, then his children had climbed it, then his grandchildren too. Sometimes now, when his daughter brought them over, they'd shin up the boughs, and at the top, they'd wave, he'd wave.

His daughter would shout *Careful!* Parents said that now. Maybe that's what was wrong with the world. Children learning to be afraid of trees.

From his bedroom, he could hear woodpeckers. He could hear buzzards call from the clouds. He could hear skylarks, and at night, owls and foxes. The clatter of pheasants and the shots from the hunt. In the mornings, sparrows sparked up out the honeysuckle when the postman brushed the hedge trying to pick his way round the glass and weeds.

Beyond the treetops there was nothing but the Downs. He could see the fields change with the seasons from his bed. The sheep track had been tarmacked. He watched fewer tractors and more fast cars go by. Sometimes, people flung themselves off Mount Caburn. Used to be army training. Now it was rich people's thrills.

171

He thought about his wife. She'd been bedbound, but he'd had no patience. He didn't understand it then. Left her sister to nurse her while he was busy in the garden. She'd tut when he'd mutter, *You can rest when you're dead.*

The longer his wife lay there giving up on life, the more Bennet went outside. Her bed had overlooked the back. She'd scold him out the window when she heard him messing with the car.

Get rid of the thing, it's ugly, John don't want it – the last proper sentence she ever said.

He thought about his mother a lot, too, in that last year of his. She'd moved back in with them, after his father had passed. She had been on lie-down, like his wife was later, like he was now.

But he'd liked his mother being in bed there. Finally, she'd been all his. Not busy fussing or doing this and that. Just lying there, quiet, in and out of sleep. He'd get back from work with stories from the Big House, so-and-so said this, so-and-so's done that, and take her tea and just sit. They didn't have to talk. They'd notice the birds. Didn't matter she was near blind. She knew each one by their sound. The tapping of yaffles. The chatter of hedge-picks and the dish-lickers' little pip-pips in the holly outside.

The burr and twang of her Sussex words came back to him, as he lay there, in that final year, like her. She would chide him now for being so *beazled*.

You sowing gape-seed again, she'd tut at him, wasting time looking out the window all day.

172

Her voice kept him soft company when he needed it. Her voice, and his old cross-eyed dog, and the thought of the boy he had been, and the man he once was, and all the people he had seen come and go, and how he didn't like the new family next door, with the kiddies that screeched and the parents who lost their rag.

He thought of that painter, sitting among the cucumbers. A famous artist, it later turned out. They sold that painting of the glasshouse as a card in the village shop, and Bennet was relieved to find he wasn't in it after all, but then wondered if it might have been nice if he was.

His late wife joined the haunt on occasion, but young, like when he married her, dancing the maypole, long plaits, yellow dress.

In those last weeks, a fever fell on him, and he spoke to his mother in her tongue. He dreamt they were in a nest together, and she was a bird.

You were speaking gibberish, his daughter said when he was awake again.

He said, No one speaks like they used to any more.

Behowtel. Another word of his mother's. Why say four words – *Be how it will* – when one would do.

★ ★ ★ ★

Four years, and the women and children still live there, in that storm-battered cottage on the winding road to the Downs.

The trees are taller, the hedgerows fuller, the pond big enough for the boys to paddle in, home to fish, newts, frogs. This summer, to her surprise, the mulberries fruited.

They have a boisterous white dog, who owns the garden, but has to wear a tracker because she likes to escape.

The beehives have gone, the elements too brutal – an apple branch fell on the hives and toppled them, bees fled or dead. But the hens are doing well. They have fifteen now. She takes in rescues, and brings them back to health. Walk past her cottage, and you'll find an honesty cupboard with eggs for sale, so huge they barely fit in the box.

Everybody knows her, and she knows everyone, and she never wants to leave, but the rent still keeps her up at night.

Her health got worse, but then better. She is stable now, on her cocktail of drugs. The struggles of her eldest got worse, then better. This garden, these animals, this air his glue. The youngest is in his last year of the little primary school. Sometimes, he walks to the shop by himself. He is safe, and proud.

Every day, she potters in the garden. There's always something to fix or build. But the Gardener speaks to her less and less now. His garden has become her garden. She's stopped finding his things. Besides, a different man's voice occupies her head now, saying words like *eviction* and *overdue rent*.

Imagination is magical, when you have lightness. But it's a malicious magic when you're living on the edge.

It's September, and she's digging again, in the half-light. Recently they've been rescuing toads off the road. The boys are worried that the chickens will eat them, so she's digging a new pond, away from their coop. The boys are very attached to their amphibians, giving them names like Jeremy Lunchbox, after the receptacles in which they brought them home.

She's digging when her spade strikes something belligerent. Automatic, to question the Gardener in her head.

A paving slab?

The Gardener doesn't answer. It isn't a paving slab. The corners aren't there.

A circle? she asks.

The shape becomes clearer, its perimeter emerging. She slips the spade below and prizes it out the ground. A large domed stone. Writing etched on top.

What is it?

He still doesn't answer. His voice has gone.

She brushes off the soil, feeling out the letters.

THIS IS BENNET'S GARDEN, it says.

★ ★ ★ ★

Winter. The end of Bennet's pillow-year. His daughter put a Christmas tree up in his room. The grandchildren hung tinsel off the bedposts. He put money into cards for them, not sure it was enough.

It was cold, but they insisted. Helped him downstairs and out the front door.

Open it then!

A large gift, nestled between the rosemary and winter pansies on the stoop. He let the grandkids unwrap it. They were excited enough not to notice he wasn't.

Ta-dah!

A large domed stone, announcing this was his garden. But it wasn't his garden. Not any more.

Thank you, it's lovely, he said.

He pulled his bobble hat over his ears and his daughter helped him back to bed.

Someone will move in here after him. Then someone after that. The next tenant, then the next. In each end, a beginning. We're all just passing through.

He might have a hope they'd all carry on the garden. But if they didn't, *behowtel*.

Still, the mouseanickels and prickleback urchins. Still, the honeysuckle and slub. Still the yesty whiffles belvering the bostal, and the children's boots stabblering in the mud. Still the age-old formula for hoping: water plus seed plus light.

A Piece, A Part, A Whole

Since they could walk, they have coveted bones. Ribs, jaws, backbones, hips, skulls, shins. Rabbit, rat, deer, sheep, badger. Owl pellets rubbed in their palms to pick out fur and beaks. A shrew left to desiccate in a tub. Birds in borax. The molar of a cow.

The Mother takes the children to the wood most days, following the greened-over train track, past the den where they hear fox cubs geckering each May, past the elderflower trees that make June birthday cordial, and the blackberry place that says it's nearly time for school and the rosehip place when the first frost comes. The oak tree you can climb, and the dead one you can't. The dip in the path where an adder once passed.

The miles and minutes of these walks are measured in snack stops and songs – folk songs, sea shanties, Cornish songs she didn't grow up with but learnt later by heart to claim her home. Songs of heroism and adventure, songs of death and doomed love.

Her sons' favourite song is 'Over the Hills and Far Away', because despite her best efforts, they have an appetite for war, and she loves it too because it comes from *Sharpe*, which her uncles let her stay up late when she was a kid and watch. It has a marching pace, so they march to it. It doesn't matter where. She has no car. No choice but for their little legs to march wherever they need to go.

Miles are nothing to them. Always, they sing.

It's a private wood, but they're allowed there. Small as woods go, but makes them feel smaller still. It's a managed wood, with coppicing and felling, so paths appear where they weren't before. She tells the children *we'll follow our noses*, as her grandmother used to say to her.

Later, she'd bring them here with sleeping bags in the middle of the night to lie between tree roots and hear the nightingales sing.

It was autumn when they first found the bones, in the bog end of a creek that they christened Bone Bay. Scuff your boot and you'd find one. So many they began bringing bags.

Found one!

Put it back. Too meaty.

An entire torso fresh in the briars. They'd always remember where it was, to go back to when the flesh had returned to the earth.

How many bones, in those early years of mothering? Bagfulls a week; hundreds, maybe more. The gleeful wonder they held for them, plucked like treasure from the undergrowth, the bog. An intact skull always the grail; sought for, rarely found. She doesn't tell them they're unlikely to find one, because the hunters keep the heads. She doesn't tell them that's why the bones are here, that this is where the cullers sling the spoils, after they've strung up the animal and cut their necks, let the blood drain out for flies, dissect it for venison, slough the skin for hides, then toss the bones for their little awe to find. The hunters were good here; no deer was just a death.

When the boys bring home their bone bags, they lay them out carefully in a row down the path, and take out the special tub of toothbrushes and toothpaste and set about scrubbing them clean. The mother is strict about the meatiness. They must get rid of anything that could entice more flies.

Once, the Tesco delivery man steered his trolley down the path and stopped to stare at them, shaking his head.

That isn't right, he said.

One boy, bare-torsoed, wore butterfly wings. Both boys had feral tangles of hair that brushed the bones as they put their heads low. If you got close enough, there was a slight smell.

Not right, he said again, unloading the hamster food and cat food and bananas, unable to look away.

As he turned to leave, he looked right at her.

Hate to think what they'll do to you when you die,
he said.

She laughed it off. No point replying. Where the man saw death, her boys saw life. They still felt immortal in their unscarred skins.

When she dies, she knows she will be cremated, because she sees how tight they hang onto these bones.

A friend of hers needed a place to put a caravan, where he would live for a while to save money for a house. He moved into these woods, in return for helping to look after them. He was rugged and strong, like he was made to chop wood.

His caravan provided another point of orientation. Her sons were getting older. Now they rarely got lost. They carried a map in their minds of this wild place – the caravan, the rope swing, the den, Bone Bay. Sometimes, she'd sit with her friend and let the boys run off together, armed with walkie-talkies, apples and flints. He'd light a fire, and they'd make dough, and call the boys back, to twist the dough around sticks to fire-bake for lunch.

She liked these visits. She liked his voice. His stories and knowledge increased her somehow. He knew how to pick mushrooms, knew birds by their song, identified butterflies and constellations with ease. He took her to the barn owls to watch owlets shriek through flying lessons. Once, they lay amongst sheep and drank whisky as meteors showered above their heads.

Sometimes, if his son was there, he'd run around with her sons, and she'd watch them and think; yes, this is how childhood should be. For all the things I get wrong, here's one good thing. For all the things I can't give them, I can at least give them this.

One day, her friend gave her boys a skull. It was perfect; teeth still rattling in its jaw. They weren't as enthralled as she thought they'd be. It was the finding that mattered after all.

Spring comes. The woods full of bluebells. She always wishes she could capture their scent. The boys run through them to Bone Bay ahead of her, dispersing a fragrant wake.

In the months that have passed since discovering it, they have learnt to venture off the banks and into the groggy ditch itself. The bones take more cleaning, but they are better preserved here. So now it's wellies sucked into the bog-stink, and sticks to poke around until a hardness sends a tap.

The Mother sits on the fallen tree they call Buzzard Banquet, named by her caravan-friend's son. The remains of a mouse, regurgitated, lie drying out in the sun.

The Mother is tired. There is too much life in life. Her outside works so hard to keep everything inside in. She is too many people to be just one.
She picks at a pellet and watches her children. They have come into their bodies from the outside – the mouth on the breast, the finger in the hand, the tongue on an object, sensations on skin. The first cut that says, There's something beneath this.

The first earache that says, There's something inside. The first time on the toilet that says, Things can come out of you. The shock of the first time away from her that tells them, We are not the same human after all.

No wonder they are giddy. What a revelation these bones are. How they measure a femur along their own femur. Hold a triangle of pelvis to their hips. No wonder a skull is so coveted. Imagine being able to hold a mind in your hand.

If she could hold her own skull and prize it apart, she'd find a brain that has started to rot. Parts that have calcifed, turned to stone. A tumour they will say is benign. A hippocampus, shrivelled by epilepsy. But she doesn't know any of this right now. A few years will pass before she will know.

I'm fine, just tired, she says. Of course it is natural sometimes to collapse. Natural to get terrible headaches. Natural to feel a bit out of it from time to time. Natural to forget things, even words.

It's nothing, she says, I'm fine.

She has never listened to her body. Now her body is starting to shout.

In the pellet, she finds tiny mouse bones. She picks off the gunk and lays them on her palm. She calls to her children to come see, but they are busy, can't hear her, won't hear her, over their victory shouts of BONE!

At night, the Mother reads scientific journals to find interesting things for her scientific son. She is struck by some research (her laptop on the kitchen counter, the weekly bread dough set to rise, flour on computer keys, dishes all around, unopened bills) that bones are more than just bones.

A breakthrough: that bones carry memory. That a hormone called osteocalcin runs from marrow to mind. That this hormone, found in a mother mouse, crosses the placenta and forms her baby's brain. *In other words*, the article said – she forgets the name of the scientist, but she knows it was a man that picked apart this prenatal bond – *In other words, bones talk to neurons before birth*.

As you get older, like most hormones, this one ceases. Goodbye, bone mass. Hello memory loss, tiredness, frailty, depression. Imagine if you could inject it artificially. If our bones didn't grow old, maybe we wouldn't too.

She has all these things – memory loss, tiredness, low mood. Perhaps it's the fault of her bones. She was warned once that all the ballet would make them brittle. That they would crumble and break easily when she was old. She imagined them as glass panes in a greenhouse, rattling and cracking in high winds. She would rather struggle to walk than struggle, as she does now, to retain simple information, recall a word, name a face.

She watches her children stamp their wellies down to splash each other. They are laughing – until, of course, they're not. An argument breaks out, as it always does. The youngest slips over, his welly boot falls off.

I hate you! he screams. Muuuuuuum!

She ignores it. Can't face them. Too tired. Besides, they might figure it out. Sometimes she worries they'll kill each other. But they always find a ceasefire of sorts in the woods.

She picks a skeleton leaf up from the ground, and holds it to her face. Beyond the gossamer veins, they are fighting. The symmetry of the leaf is perfect. The symmetry beyond is not.

The leaf is translucent, but the light is different here. She wonders if this is what it's like on the other side. What devastating sweetness to hold a window that is also a shroud. A one-way mirror, she always watching her children, them trying to find her and seeing only themselves.

Rooks scatter suddenly. The youngest looks up. The eldest tries to kick him while he's not looking, but his foot gets stuck in the mud.

She would like to live long enough to see their fighting become something like love.

How long will they have together, the three of them? They believe she's immortal, as all mothers must be. But they will get older, and she'll age with them – slowly at first, then impossibly fast – and they will suddenly realise, with a shock, that she is mortal, and that one day she too will be buried in the ground.

When that day comes, they will see, like the Tesco man, the fear, not the wonder, of bones.

But for now, they are fractious and bog-deep, firing out wrath and flailing limbs. And there she is, walking through the blue-bells, putting the mouse parts and leaf in her bag.

She will lift the bootless one, crying, out the mud. The treasures he has collected will have fallen out his bag. His trousers will be soaking, and he'll have to walk home in his pants, and he'll get cold and start wheezing, without his inhaler, and she will take off her jumper and pull the arms up his legs, and the eldest will laugh at these ridiculous trousers and the other will yell at him, Stop laughing it's your fault.

They will walk home, and it will take forever, and there won't be singing or snacks.

They will walk home, and she will start ranting, in a way she can't control, about how fed up she is of their fighting, how they don't hurt each other, it's her they hurt, HER.

But they will not hear, cannot hear, still bickering, adding her upset to each other's blame, and she'll storm off ahead of them, and the day will be ruined, they have ruined the day, and then she will hate herself for being angry at them, for not holding it together, for not being a good role model for containing their hurts.

Is this normal for brothers, or is it just her sons? Where has she gone wrong? Her gran liked to tell her, It's what boys are meant to do. She's too sensitive, people tell her. Just let 'em fight it out.

When they get home, she'll run a bath for the youngest. There will be mud left around the tub. The bog-rank clothes will stay on the kitchen floor until she gets round to it. If money wasn't tight, she'd just throw them away.

The eldest will storm up to his bedroom. She knows he will be lost to her, to anyone, for a while. He can explain a Black Hole and also become one. A painful mirror for her reflection to stare back.

She will start cooking, she'll make lasagne, he likes that. She'll open the fridge, forget why she opened it, lay her head in the cheese drawer, and cry.

Then it will all be okay. She will hold them as the dinner is cooking. She will hold them and kiss them, saying sorry again and again. Explaining where her anger had come from, and what she could have done differently to manage it, to keep control. Take responsibility, say she should have come when they first called for her. If she'd have stepped in then, it wouldn't have escalated as it had.

She'll ask them for their own reflections. They'll say sorry – begrudging to each other, tenderly to her. And then they'll eat dinner, and watch *Lego Masters* together, and connect again in wonder about how little bricks make extraordinary things.

At bedtime, she'll remember the leaf again.

Hey boys, I forgot – I found this.

They'll hold it up to their faces and marvel as they notice the light.

The Mother knows now what she should have told the Tesco man.

She'd have said –

I want them to know me, beyond these bones I'll die with. Nothing unsaid between us. Nothing unknown. Nothing left rotting, to scrub with duty or guilt.

I don't want them to feel they have to look after me. Scrape lichen, take flowers, trim grass.

I want them to know that I am always all around them, and that it's beautiful, that haunting, and they must never be afraid.

That there is divinity and miracle, if you look for it, in the sacred inexplicable of this earth.

She'd have told him –

If there's one thing I can do to save them, it is to pour a deity into this land.

One day I will not be here, and you, my loves, still will.

If there is grace in the beyond, then know this: I will always be here, in whatever way you choose.

In the air inside the air of you. The light inside the light.

The wind that shakes the rooks free. Soil in your fingers. A river, a leaf.

I will rest wherever you rest me – a piece, a part, a whole.

In loss lies love, to increase you. Increase each other. Please. In these woods. In this bog.

The boys go to bed. She takes the skeleton leaf and slips it inside the pages of a book.

Maybe they'll find it again. Maybe they won't.

On the Other Side of Silence

It's six in the morning when we arrive at the hospital. The first time in years we have been on our own. Without the boys, we are a daughter and a mother. My mothering, your grandmothering, on hold.

I check onto the ward. You hesitate.

I'll be fine, I say. You can go.

I know, you say.

Knowing I mean: please stay.

The last time we'd been together like this was also in hospital. Again because someone needed to drive. You were the patient that time, me the driver. Dawn again, but winter, still dark.

I parked. We got out. Then – Look! It can't be! – strolling towards us, through the half-light – a stag.

I waited while you had your surgery. I wanted to go in with you, but wasn't allowed. Your eyes clamped open. A local anaesthetic. You'd had to watch the scalpel come towards you, slice your eyes.

They brought you back to me, blood still streaming.

Is it bad, you'd asked me, trembling.

No. You're beautiful, Mumeroo. Come here.

My surgery's just a day procedure, but a general anaesthetic is involved. We laugh – as I try to get comfortable on a bed with no pillows, but by a window at least – about the last time I had an operation, getting my tonsils out when I was five. We laugh, as we always laugh about this story – how you watched your compliant, well-behaved little daughter start violently attacking the nurse.

I was terrified of needles! No way was she getting near me!

You laugh, still incredulous at how I'd transformed.

You were really kicking her! You tried to get off the bed and escape!

The nurse gave up in the end, and gave me yellow medicine, which knocked me out long enough to put the anaesthetic in. I remember waking up, my throat feeling like gravel. They removed my adenoids as well as my tonsils, so everything I drank came out my nose.

I tell you I remember you being there.

> They were wheeling me down a corridor. I was just coming round. I remember saying 'Mum!' And there you were.

I'm last on the schedule for the morning's procedures. A small ward of seven women, all loud. Some awaiting operations, others recovering. My neighbour is broadcasting gory details down her phone.

> So they cut it out – yeah, the cyst – and they couldn't believe it. I mean, they knew it was big, but it was double the size of the scan. Guess how big! No . . . higher . . . higher . . .

Eleven centimetres, I mouth to you.

While you were in the café, I'd heard this story three times.

> Eleven centimetres! the woman says triumphantly. They showed me a photo! Bigger than a fist!

Another woman is being examined by the consultant who is running through reams of medical history on her chart. More diagnoses than a medical dictionary. The consultant keeps calling her Christine. She keeps correcting him – 'Chris'.

I had a termination when I was a kid, if that's relevant, she says.

Okay, Christine.

Chris. But my partner is a woman now, she says.

My turn comes to be wheeled into surgery. You look at me seriously.

I love you, you say.

I roll my eyes.

Don't start.

Then in a stupid voice –

Fine . . . I wuuv 'oo too.

Long corridor.
White corridor.
Rushing.

Mum?

Rushing white air.
White light.

Mum? Are you there?

Conscious. Unconscious. Dissolving. No body. Just atoms of light.

Mum? Where are you?

Atoms, drifting, floating.

I'm here darling, I'm here.

Eyes open. So many faces, hands, heads.

Do you know where you are Holly, one asks too loudly.

Hospital?

Good. You had a seizure, he says.

The doctor's voice is loud and intrusive. Yours comes soft, anti-dotal, a balm.

It's going to be okay, darling. Just a seizure. Lie back and rest. You're all okay.

I'm not okay. Not for the next three days. The anaesthetic had a fight with my brain. An enormous seizure, then another, then another. They can't get them under control.

I have more and more seizures, three different types of them. Thank goodness you are there to explain how epilepsy works. The nurses, who haven't had neuro training, keep rushing over to resuscitate me when they think I've passed out.

You give them a calm heads-up when you notice I'm due one. You know, because we'll be talking, and I'll suddenly say 'Shhhhh'. Everything gets very loud before a seizure. Very heavy, very bright, very loud.

I want to tell you that line from *Middlemarch* about silence, but I'll have to find it later, my brain's too gone.

More seizures. Different nurses. It's dark now. It's night-time, or maybe it's not.

You're still there.

I'm there and I'm not there. I'm in and out. I'm on and off.

In my arm pumps a line of pharmaceuticals, stopping electrical activity in my brain.

It's a bit like a coma, I hear you whisper.

Don't be dramatic, I say, or I think.

The drugs knock my adulthood out of me. The world is sensation, colour and smell. The blue curtain around me waves softly. I watch it for – seconds? hours? – entranced. I hold my hands to my face to inhale the hand gel, finding wonderment, euphoria.

Smell it! I say.

I put my hands on your nose.

Smell it, Mum! It's so nice!

You laugh. I get the giggles. I can't stop laughing. I'm an infant. I'm off my face.

One of the nurses transforms into a squirrel, squirrelling about my bed with little squirrelly paws.

I suck in my cheeks and can't look at you because we'll both start laughing – me because my nurse is a squirrel, you because I'm being so weird – and both of us because it's joyous to experience this – to be so wholly part of someone, so part of their bones, that without a word or glance, your mouths rise in unison and both of you explode, without knowing why, into laughs.

A different nurse assumes we are sisters. People have been making this mistake half my life. The pride I used to feel, that our faces showed my feelings. We are the same! Yes! The same! Me and Mum!

But this time I frown, because the maths isn't good here.

Does that mean I look . . . sixty?

The Mauritian nurse laughs. I know she's Mauritian, because one night she sat next to me and told me stories about her family back home. In the midst of the brain-haze, Mauritian words floated back to me from old housemates I once had, and I started speaking to her in Creole. She thought I was having another seizure, until she deciphered her mother tongue and clapped her hands.

You don't look sixty, she says. Your mum just looks young.

It's true – you've always looked naturally youthful. No make-up, no potions. Just you. You are so beautiful, and you have absolutely no sense of it. I wish you had a partner, someone good, someone magical, who told you every single day that you were beautiful, till you believed it too.

Did I stop you finding that person? In my persistence to keep you mine, my mum? Will I be alone too, for always, like you and your mother before?

We wouldn't give up our freedom for anything. Not for anyone. That's what we always conclude.

Unless they were very, very rich and about to die, we laugh.

What do you do while I'm sleeping in the hospital? You don't go anywhere. You wait for me to wake up. To speak softly to me, through my confusion. To hold my hand and tell me again it's all okay.

Sometimes, you tell stories about when I was little. You tell me the story of my first trip to the beach.

> You were so scared of the sand. I had to carry you.
> You cried when your feet touched the ground.

Sometimes, when I'm sleeping, I can you feel you in the distance, like there's hundreds of miles between my sleep and my skin.

Sometimes I can hear you, though I know you have left for the night. A voice that's inside me, and far away from me at the same time.

> I've made God out of my mother, I think. Or my mother out of God.

And it's beautiful. I wouldn't change it. It's true.

In my sleep-not-sleep, I see you in scenes like paintings.

You – walking to our mine down the garden, bedsheets billowing, daisies nodding as you pass.

You – giving your sheepskin gloves to a homeless man one bitterly cold winter. Even though your fingers, even in summer, were always numb. We didn't know you had a circulation disorder. We thought you had a superpower, because you could take things out the oven with bare hands. You were always cold, but there was nothing but sweet warmth inside you, which you always gave so easily away. When ice formed on the inside of our bedroom window, we snuggled up in your bed, and your blood became our blood, like before we were born.

You – on the road in Brighton, by the side of a just-collapsed young man. Busy Christmas shoppers stepping over him, assuming he was drunk. You clearing the space around him, even stopping cars. You on your knees in the puddles, talking gently and stroking his head. He came round, frightened, wide-eyed. You soothed him tenderly, helped him to his feet. Held him. Spoke to him with reassurance.

I'm diabetic, I need sugar, he said.

Someone else brought him chocolate. A shop security guard brought an umbrella out. The rain was torrential. The man had no coat. He was on his way to a shelter, he told you. He lit a cigarette. You stood close by him, holding the umbrella, even though I knew you'd hate the smell of the smoke.

I held the boys' hands. We were watching you.

I said, Never forget your nan is the greatest human
on this Earth.

For a while, at university, I saw a therapist. My eating disorder
had reared its starving vomiting head. After rattling off my
usual CV of dysfunction and trauma (therapy bored me, I'd
never had a breakthrough, never had a good therapist, not since
I was sixteen), this particular therapist said something new to
me. Something I immediately told him was wrong.

You have unreasonably polarised your parents. You
father isn't a monster. Your mother isn't a perfect
saint.

I guess some people might have corrected him: 'You haven't met
my father'. But I wanted to scream at him, 'You haven't met my
mum'.

I haven't idolised you. I'm not the type. I've looked for reasons
to hate you. They're simply not there. Get everyone who knows
you in one room, and all of them would say the same as me.

But my main disagreement with this therapist – I did the manda-
tory six sessions, then never went back – was that, even if I had

elevated you in my estimation, how can that be anything but a wonderful thing? Idolatry is only dysfunctional when you fail to see the whole person. Wipe a cloth over their idiosyncrasies and flaws.

But I see the whole of you, know the whole of you, and my opinion remains constant. Your goodness has never been an unattainable bar above my head. A bar to beat myself with when I fell short. There is no bar. It isn't in you to present one. Your goodness has never been a calibration, a standard, for me. A form of being – not a form of measurement. The fact you are blind to your own goodness is precisely why it emanates through.

I tried to explain to him:

> You don't get into a beautiful, well-made bed at night
> and think, this bed is so perfectly made, I'd better try
> to perfectly sleep. You just sleep. Sometimes well,
> sometimes not well. But the bed is there holding you,
> keeping you warm, just the same.

I leave hospital, high on benzos. The intensity of being outside. We listen to birdsong. I google that line from *Middlemarch*, as you carefully drive us home.

> If we had a keen vision and feeling of all ordinary
> human life, it would be like hearing the grass grow

and the squirrel's heart beat, and we should die of
that roar which lies on the other side of silence.

That's beautiful, you say.

Squirrel, I laugh.

And then we come home, and real life breaks in again. Our
motherhood and grandmotherhood must resume. Dishes, dog,
cat, hens, homework. You insisting I recover. Me insisting I'm
fine.

I close the door I'd opened to you in hospital, when I was a
cluster of atoms, floating over the world.

Honestly, I'm fine, I can manage.

I know, you reply.

Knowing this time I don't mean: stay.

Why do I always do this? Keep my daughter door closed to you.
Pretend I don't need you. Push you away.

At some point – I don't know when, but as a young child I was aware of it – there fell over my daughterhood a kind of spell.

As if an evil fairy appeared at my cot one day and – after the other fairies had bestowed their nice gifts – it had leaned in close and tapped its dark wand on my forehead.

The mother you've been born to is the greatest gift of all, it hissed. *But if you ever truly acknowledge that, then your mother will die.*

I had my evidence. Not just my books from the library, in which Nice Mothers always died. But in your many near-fatal experiences. In our home, on a tube train, mid-flight. Each time was like the wicked fairy reminding me:

See? She's mortal. Extinguishable. She glows like a candle, but I'll snuff her out. Remember what I warned you. Don't get too close.

So I stick to my policy of stubborn non-sentimentality. Squirm when you say nice things. Retreat when you get close. Resist your affection, return hugs only fleetingly. Say Alright, alright, when you declare your love. Crack jokes. Take the piss. Roll my eyes at you.

To profess my love for you would mean accepting you were mortal. But you're going to live forever, right? No need for mush.

Of course we were always laughing in the hospital. But when I was asleep, did you cry?

One day, your death will be my death. And if I acknowledge how much I need you in this life, I will have to acknowledge what I will lose when you're gone. If I began to say out loud what you mean to me, I wouldn't be able to stop.

But I know that you know it. You feel the felt-but-unsaid. You don't collude with my withdrawal – you openly, expressively, unconditionally love me, and always have. But you don't judge me for not saying it. You understand why I can't.

I don't say what I want to say, because – like George Eliot – I would die of that roar on the other side. It isn't just you. The people I'm closest to I keep the most distant. Perhaps something is broken in me. I've never got my head around love.

Fairies or no fairies, my greatest gift is my mother. You know me beyond words. You know me better than myself.

And now you are driving, alone, back to Cornwall. You must be exhausted. My withdrawals are cruel. But I have to insist on managing without you. Like rehearsals, or drills, for the day you'll be gone.

I sit in my garden, with the bats, in the half-light, waiting for your text to say you're safely home. Lean my head back, on the sofa made of pallets. Watch the last of the swallows, the first of the stars.

I'm high, and exhausted. They've changed my daily meds. The new drugs are potent, the adjustment brings haze. It's summer, and everything is growing. I stare at my garden. I can feel it hum. I can hear the pulse of a train in the distance. It stays in my ears. It's the heartbeat of the world.

Your message arrives. You're home again. *Jiggety-jig*, as you always say.

I message back.

> Thank you for everything. I'm so grateful. I know I don't say it enough – but I love you.

Because I'm a coward, who can write things I can't say.

One day, you'll die, and your death will be my death. And none of this will have protected me from that roar. Not my distance, not my rehearsals, not my piss-takes. These meaningless talismans I hold against that curse.

Let's spend more time together. Just the two of us.

Let our daughterhoods, motherhoods, grandmotherhoods unfurl.

No distractions. Definitely no hospitals.

Let's go to the beach. You won't have to carry me. I'm not scared of sand any more.

Let's own our mortality and revel in the finite. We are two women, made of stories and bones. We can't do much about these bodies we move in. But we can make new stories. I will find those words. Find ways to say everything I want to tell you. There is no wicked fairy. There is no dark wand.

Let's laugh. Oh it's beautiful, that laughter. Let's keep laughing together, right to the end. So when I'm there, saying goodbye to you at your funeral, I'll suddenly giggle, and know you're giggling too.

Best Man

They think I'm the stripper. A fair enough mistake – low-cut leotard, stilettos, blonde wig. It's hot, but I pull a cardi out my supplies bag and button it over my chest.

The small-city sports bar is rowdy. Our group of wrestlers is the rowdiest of all. I weave through bodies with a sticky tray of Jagerbombs, already too exhausted for the night that's just begun.

I pass you a glass.

Down the hatch.

Cheers.

We screw up our faces and stick out our tongues. Beneath the fake-tan frivolity, we are old.

The Brother and the Sister are adults. They have their own adult worlds. One of them's about to get married. The other's about to leave a twelve-year relationship and start a new life. The Brother will be thirty soon and knows everything. The Sister knows nothing any more. There was a time once when there were categories. Now she swings like a pendulum in the perpetual inbetween.

Alright Stag? I say, before sneezing.

Alright Best Man? you reply.

You pull me in. My arms don't fit round you. Two years younger than me, but four times the size. Our nicknames, Little Big and Big Little. I pull away suddenly, slimy with glitter from your chest. You laugh and daub me with more of it, slapping it onto my cheeks.

Stop! They already think I'm a hooker!

Who?!

The men at the bar.

A MILF snot fetish. Niche.

God is it bad?

I find a tissue and dab my nose.

Much better, you say. Now you're a cokehead stripper.

Fuck off, it's allergies!

It's what happens when I'm stressed. Pulling this off has been stressful – a stag party for my brother, in a city I didn't know, and a bunch of guys who didn't trust a thirty-two-year-old mother to bring the requisite level of debauch. Okay so I'd drawn up a spreadsheet and circulated a timetable and task list in advance. But if I couldn't be the 'Man' in my title, then I should try to live up to the 'Best'.

Our wrestlers are back at the bar already. It's going to be a long, messy night.

The Brother and the Sister are wrestlers. Eight and ten, and the Brother is obsessed. He gets the videos from Woolworths on his birthdays, or sometimes their gran tapes it off TV. Sunday mornings he shouts, WrestleMania! and they pile onto his bed. Even their mum joins in, striving to be the father she sees her sporty rough-n-tumble son needs.

The Brother always plays the All-American golden boy, Bret 'Hitman' Hart. The Sister is anyone except the Undertaker. When he makes his ghoulish entrance, she's so scared she can't watch.

The violence on the videos isn't real. It's make-believe, choreo-graphed, like dance. But sometimes, she's terrified. The illusion so accurate. The pain so believable. Flashbacks. Her heart in her throat.

The violence when they play wrestling isn't real either. But sometimes, something flips. Maybe not for the Brother, whose heart is made of lightness and giggles. But the Sister is darker. She likes the hurt.

These are the last of the years when she'll be bigger than him. Soon, she'll be small and he'll be big, like their dad.

More bars, more drinks, more banter, more games I come up with and dares I don't. I watch you and your friends dance like idiots. I watch the fake tan shimmer and streak the muscles below your skin.

I'm tired. You're tired too, I think. But we've both always been good at pretend.

We end up, of course, at a strip club. Not on my itinerary. Neither of us want to go in. Dragged in by your friend, who has taken over as a self-appointed, more typical best man. It's weird and musty inside, like the working men's club where I first learned to dance.

If I looked like a stripper in the sports bar, I definitely look like one now. Men come up to me. I sneeze repeatedly and never leave your side. One extortionately priced and awkward whisky later, a few of us decide to leave.

We stumble home to white Russians and *The Big Lebowski*. Both of us know every line. The strip-club renegades roll home full of stories, and we pass out on various surfaces to sleep.

What stag night would I have wanted to give you? One in which we travelled back in time.

To our mine at the bottom of the garden, digging up fossils and coins.

To the baths we shared for hours as children, the cork mat between us like a table on the rim, the stage for our farmyard animals and bath toys and bubble whisks. Unfolding toilet roll tubes and soaking them in the water, then forming the papery mush into nappies and singing *Pull your pants down Paddy Ashdown* and laughing, when you couldn't have been older than five.

To the café we'd play chess and scrabble in. That time you beat me with LYNX for sixty-four points.

To the beach, as kids, with your metal detector, then later, night swims, freezing and sloshed.

To the Italian restaurant we worked in as teenagers, bringing home free pizza at midnight and watching people sleep on *Big Brother* on TV.

To that heavy-metal dive bar we used to go to, playing drunken pat-a-cake with our hands in our shoes.

To Prague on your eighteenth birthday, a surprise trip to see Bob Dylan, our hero, who played all his worst songs and monotonally sucked.

To the Isle of Wight, where you chased me into the Channel and dumped me in, in all my clothes, and we resolved to train for a marathon, which I ended up running alone.

To our childhood kitchen, singing together. How quickly you mastered the guitar.

To the bed we shared every Christmas Eve, so we could wake each other up at dawn, to find magic and chocolate coins in our stockings. We kept that ritual well into our teens, when Christmas began with you punching me repeatedly and screaming *Wake up you grinch!* in my face.

I'd take us back to all the times we've got the giggles and contagiously, inappropriately, deliciously, laughed. Like that awkward dinner when we heard everything as inuendo. Like that bizarre funeral, when we had to eat our fists.

You have always made me laugh more than anyone. The only person who can help when I'm depressed. Maybe, if we didn't live two hundred miles apart now, I wouldn't have been on anti-depressants my whole adult life.

I'd take us back to my first memory: the day you were born. I was only two, so the memory is fleeting – a few seconds at most – of walking into a toy shop that was busy and everything seemed up very high. I don't remember the rest – buying you a teddy, arriving at the hospital, seeing you for the very first time.

The Brother and the Sister have always had each other. They can't remember a time without the other one around.

Still – sibling relationships are innately elusive. No lightning strike of love, no unconditional bond, no chemical attachment, or deep-rooted need. Rather, an arrangement, a fingers-crossed experiment, in which two strangers with shared parentage spend enough time together to create something that resembles love.

Resembles – because the first love is mother-love, and nothing can ever feel like that. And so, through your sibling, you discover there are different types of love – complex, conditional, with undertones of hate. A relationship you have to build brick by brick together, laying memory and experience onto genes and routines.

For the eldest, the newborn sibling is Other. The Sister has to remember to enfold the Brother into her world, the way you have to remember to add currants to a cake.

For the youngest, there is no Other. There are no currants. Only one big cake.

Such different people. It seems remarkable they got here. Their love has been hard-forged, well-tested, fraught. But something clicked on the other side of childhood. After the Sister left home, it was like meeting for the first time.

From then on, they were so close, so similar. Finishing each other's sentences. Paralysing each other with jokes. Dancing, bickering, mind-reading, banter, affection, rituals and hugs. People who didn't know them assumed they were *together* together, and were envious when corrected, saying they wished they had siblings like that.

Of course she would be his best man.

He has been the best man she knows, all his life.

> Where are we going, you ask hungover the next morning.
>
> A surprise.
>
> And I'm wearing this because . . .

I sing –

Cos you'll look sweet / upon the seat / of a bicycle made for—

Oh . . . fuck.

—twoooooooooo!

The bike-hire place is near the station. Five tandems await. Everyone groans. I'm no longer best man, but an evil matron, punishing schoolboys who would rather be in bed.

Cycling with a hangover is hard. Tandem cycling, *without* a hangover, is hard. Hungover tandeming, therefore, is near-impossible. We manage a metre down the seafront then fall off.

We try different configurations – me on the front, because I'm less hungover. But I'm also a terrible cyclist with no spatial awareness. So we swap. Which means you're on the front as we pedal down the promenade, your long wig and flouncy skirts blowing back at me in the breeze.

It's busier than I thought it would be. A kind of little festival taking place on the lawns. People laugh and point as we pass them. I stop pedalling because I'm pissing myself laughing as you moan and grimace, hamming up the swears.

We stop for a pint and watch a ukelele orchestra. It's eleven in the morning and everyone else is old. One look at each other and we're laughing. It's a gift we have. One I hope we'll never lose. Without saying a word, we have the same image in our heads of the eccentric old teacher who taught us guitar at school.

Sure enough, you begin the impression of him, and we lie back on the grass, strumming imaginary guitars.

The Brother and the Sister are both musical. She plays viola, they both play piano, he plays guitar. Both always singing, often together, trying harmonies. He writes his own songs and starts bands, a rock god, approached by a label while he's still in his teens. She's a classicist, playing politely with orchestras. He performs at bars and drives crowds wild.

Like everything, the Sister works hard at her music while the Brother's a natural who can do it in his sleep. She's trained to be good at it, slaving through scales, panicking about exams, while he's largely self-taught. She has perseverance. He has a gift.

Opposites, yes – but it brings them together. Musical notes wrap round the helix of their genes. They make each other mixtapes, go to gigs together, argue about this or that album, this or that band. For a while, she's a music journalist. He has his own music radio show. They record an album together, his songs, his music, her background vocals and strings.

Their home is full of music, and their mother is happy, because it means the three of them are full of music too. Not the music of the steel town – lighters, sirens, ringpulls, punches, screams.

A whole new score, orchestrating all around them – chatter and laughter, seagulls and waves. The buzz of her children's creativity. The hum of the hot-water pipes she laid with her own hands.

The Brother and Sister fall asleep to the song of her sewing machine, and wake up in the morning to the gentle thud of her kneading bread.

More beers, more banter, more tandeming. Crazy golf. The betting shop. Deep-fried food. On the train home, you fall asleep against the window. The woman opposite us stares at you for a while then suppresses a giggle as you absently pull up a bra strap. She whispers to me, He looked so peaceful that I couldn't work out what was wrong with the overall vibe.

You have always held that ability to be peaceful. A word that has never described me.

We carry the same past, but you have bigger shoulders. Your heart is far softer than mine. You are built like a tank, but I've been in more scraps than you have. I got the tattoos and scars, not you.

You love so intuitively, so loyally, so openly. You still love mum like an affectionate infant, even though you're twice her size. You still curl up with her and make her stroke your hair, while I struggle to give her a hug.

Like everything, at love you're a natural. For me, it is complicated work. I've never got it right. But I'm so proud that you have.

How have you done it – remained soft, against the odds? Maybe, in our partners, you've looked for mothers and I for fathers. Your pattern a blessing, mine a curse.

For a while, the Brother and the Sister didn't like each other. Adolescence cleaved them, like a chasm through a rock. Him on one side, funny, cool and popular, her on the other, serious and odd. Him all Body, her all Mind.

At eleven, he shot up and was suddenly a man-child – tall, tough, athletic, muscular, strong. Dazzling on pitches with kicks and catches, dazzling on stage with his gravelly voice and guitar. Boys wanted to be him, girls wanted to be with him. Even her friends in the sixth form would flirt.

He made no attempt to disguise his testosterone, and nobody told him he should – hands always casually down his pants, wearing a T-shirt saying: Masturbation Is Not A Crime. Writing a song about losing his virginity and playing it to the family, rhyming 'attic' and 'prophylactic'. The Sister never went through puberty. She didn't even know what prophylactic meant.

The bigger he got, the smaller she became. His physical presence and easy charisma filled her with hate. His swagger, pierced eyebrow, sweary T-shirts, black-painted bedroom, bottle-bleached hair. The way he could rattle off quotes by Salinger and Nietzsche, cultivating arguments against anything she said. She worked so hard to achieve things that came to him easily. She was sensible and did all the right things. He was cheeky but charming, breaking rules, never caught.

How could she hurt him now? She couldn't. He was too big for her. Too strong, too immune.

She had to find a new way to hurt. She ripped the skin of her lips and fingers, making them bleed, till she almost passed out. And then the calm came, that sweet blank peace she needed. She'd tie elastic bands around the wound until the blood stopped, only feeling satisfied when she counted the tissue squares drenched in her blood.

The wedding comes. Sun, flowers, beautiful. A picturesque village full of family and friends. But I'm crying in my hotel room, trying to get ready. Feeling that volcano bubbling in me again. I'm crying because I have two dresses, both suddenly ugly. I feel fat and hideous. Can't leave the room.

I text you.

Yes it's all about me, I say. *Me me me. On your special day.*

Somewhere, I have two toddlers. My eldest will be anxious. He doesn't like change, new places, crowds.

I should be happy. Everyone's happy. But I'm split into versions of myself I can't integrate into one whole.

I can't be your best man, and get out there, showtime jazz hands, while also being your sister, who is finally realising I'm letting you go, and also be a mother, with tiny children who are struggling, and also be myself, a version I'm happy with, in a body I can stand to be photographed and filmed.

It's not about you Pook, it's all good, just get yourself here yeah?

I know it's the wrong dress as soon as I join you in the foyer. Too late now. Here comes the car. I'm by your side.

The Sister knows its love because she'd do anything to protect the Brother, even when he really pisses her off. When things are difficult, as things were in those early years, she would shield him with her body and not let anything bad close. She would die for him. She knew that. She didn't have to like him to know love.

As a young child, he was so scared of things. He wouldn't go anywhere, even upstairs, on his own. He seemed so vulnerable, inside and outside. A misguided mullet that he named Long

219

Colin, an imaginary friend called Merv, an eye patch over his lazy-eye glasses, having nightmares and creeping into their mother's bed.

The Sister worried that her brother was in the same category as her, their auntie, their gran. How would he grow up and move into the MAN category?

What if he didn't grow tough enough?

What if he *did* grow tough?

She knows now that the Brother also saw categories. He knew like her: Men/Bad, Women/Good. That for the Brother, as for her, his body betrayed him. His exterior and interior misaligned.

She wonders what it was like for him to be raised in that all-female coven. How deeply he felt the pressure to become a Good Man. How hard he had to work to never slip steelwards. To never raise his voice, his hand.

I stand next to you at the front of the church. I swear I can hear your heart. The organist plays 'Here Comes The Sun' again. A third time. A fourth time. Where's your bride? Nervous chatter ripples round the church pews. The photographer captures you and I giggling, then again, both pulling a worried face.

Finally the doors open. The bells stop ringing. Everybody turns. You turn.

I don't turn. I'm watching you, my brother.

The love on your face fills and breaks and fills me again.

You can do things I will never do: love. Shed cruelty. Forgive.

What existential landmines littered the fields of our becoming. You skipped nimbly through them. I trod on every one.

Your bride arrives, and I leave you. She is so beautiful. Outside and in. You both laugh and cry throughout the ceremony. How beautiful, how magical, to marry your best friend.

What would have happened, if they'd stayed in the steel town? Who would the Brother and Sister have become?

Their dad kept tropical fish in buzzing fishtanks and the best thing was when he took them to the aquarium shop. Low-lit and hot, soft humming, bubbles rising gently through the glass. Fish of all shapes and colours. Piranhas in a pool at the back.

There was a tiny shark.

> Shouldn't it be massive, she'd asked the aquarium man.

> Fish grow to the size of their tank, he'd said.

A perfect wedding. Everybody said so. The party at the cute village hall, all ages on the dancefloor till midnight. It was the last time the family was all together. A beautiful thing, to unite us all like that.

My speech was a corker. How wonderful to have your sister as best man, they all said.

He's *my* best man, I reply to them.

And he is. He is.

You are. You are.

She Had Label in Her Pocket

A year after your gran dies, you find them: six pink Post-its, documenting, in miniature, a day out to London, just you and her.

You were too young to remember it properly. Instead, it *became* a memory later on, the way things do after years of retelling, the photographs revisited till they form a stop-motion film, playing over and over to create a memory-like narrative, real enough, in your mind.

In this photofilmmemory, you are four with stubby bunches, a tomboy with red braces holding up your jeans, holding your gran's hand at various London landmarks. With her white hair, twinset, and smiling false teeth, it's a shock to work out she was only a little older than you are now.

Since she died, you avoid anything she left you. But the Post-it Notes are different. Small enough to face. You lay them out and shuffle them, each a bone in the story's skeleton, until the anatomy looks right. Until it's both 2017, and you're without her, and 1987, and you're in London with her again. Until another map grafts over the top of them, of the London you discovered later as a student. A cartography aged four, another aged twenty. Your gran forty, then sixty, now gone.

A momentous adventure, condensed into six small rectangles, distilled into black biro facts in her neat hand. Facts separated, or connected, by quick dashes and arrows – symbols, like lines between dates on a gravestone, of everything left out.

St Pancras   Liverpool St   Tower Hill
Holly learnt to look for Line colours and follow them

You remember – or do you? It's the briefest of glimpses – her finger on the Tube map tracing the lines. She had always decoded the world for you, making the unfathomable make sense. Once, when you were terrified of needles, she brought a syringe home from her job at the doctor's and showed you, with an orange, how little it went in and how little it brought out.

Tower:
Jewel House – Ravens – White Tower (Armoury) – Cannons
– Wild Boar – Bear Trap – Axe – Elephant Armour –
Japanese Things – Bloody Tower (Princes Murdered There)

You remember – not from this time, but later – her telling you the story of the princes in the Tower. Murdered children, murderous men. The tricksiness, the mystery. Their names on the wall. This was her favourite period of history. As a child, you understood more about Tudor society than you did about your own.

Beefeater – Crisp

You remember – no you don't, you have no memory of it, but she repeated the story often enough – the beefeater who took a shine to you, something involving him stealing a crisp. A little metal yeoman, that she bought in the shop for you, still stands on your mantlepiece, a talisman, tangible, confirming as concrete the photofilmmemory you have made in your mind.

Climbed a lot of stairs – Got lost a lot

You wish you could remember her climbing stairs. But later, her body made this impossible, and that's all you remember now. You do, however, remember getting lost a lot. Not on this trip maybe, but all the others you went on. Getting lost was her speciality. Her mantra: FOLLOW YOUR NOSE. Although she was never lost at all, you now see that. She pretended to be lost, so you could believe you made her found.

She was trying to teach you to never fear lostness. But in London as a student, that was always the case.

Sat by Tower Riverside for lunch – Tower Bridge and HMS Belfast. Fed thousands sparrows. Got boat at Tower Pier. Went up river to almost Westminster (20 mins) – past Southwark Bridge – London Bridge (where we said rhyme about it falling down) – saw St Pauls Cathedral (talked of Royal Wedding) – the Monument (talked of Fire of London and Plague)

South of the river was your adulting territory. When you first moved to London, you lived near Tate Modern for a while, then later on the wharf by Tower Bridge. You worked at a pub with an abusive manager on the river and life-modelled for an art school by Waterloo. Drank and danced in clubs under London

Bridge railway arches. Went to Borough Market at closing time and charmed sellers into giving you free bags of food then sat and ate it with your homeless friend David, talking about politics, under Blackfriars Bridge.

You wouldn't remember being four and walking there with her, as she brought the area's history to visceral life. For years as a child, you had recurring nightmares about the Plague. You wonder if this is where they began.

She came with your auntie-mum once to visit you. You went to the Rothko exhibition at the Tate. She hated it, berating it loudly, to annoy the viewers looking in awe at the towering paint. You crossed the Millennium Bridge. She didn't like that either. Then you all sat by St Paul's.

Did she talk about your day together there, fifteen years before? Was she thinking – as she watched you, grown up and twenty, a streetwise city-thing, messy hair and skater clothes and the nose ring she vehemently disliked – how once your little hand held her hand, and you sang nursery rhymes, a thousand sparrows at your feet?

Had chocolate eclairs (Holly reminded me it was rubbish food but added it was lovely)

What a precocious four-year-old you were. Your mother had raised you so well. The only sweets you were normally allowed were from the health-food shop, jewels of pineapple and papaya, chewy banana chips, dried apple rings you slipped round your thumb. Everything your mother cooked was handmade and healthy. Your gran quickly spotted a gap where you could love her, piling you full of biscuits, cakes, ice cream, sweets.

Festival Pier — walked along South Bank — watched artists
— played on modern stone sculptures — folksy music buskers

When you were twenty-one, studying full-time, working two bar jobs, battling panic attacks and bulimia, you never slept. So at one or two in the morning, you would put on your rollerblades and glide up and down the Southbank, just you, a few homeless and drunks, the mayor's office security guards shooing you away.

Insomnia runs in the family. Perhaps because trauma does too. So a few hours later, when you got back to your student room, you'd call your gran, because you knew she'd be up. She'd have slept in her armchair for a bit, maybe with the Australian cricket on, and she'd have got up and started pottering before the sun.

She'd pick up, say *744063?* in the posh voice she reserved for the phone.

Hi Gran, it's me.

Hello, treasure! How are you?

You'd give anything to hear that again.

> *Passed book market — watched people going into National*
> *Theatre when they rang performance bell (we talked of the*
> *plays)*

The book market on the South Bank is still there. You always go when you're in town. You have found books there in special old editions, and a painting of Cornwall when you needed it most. The first time you went inside the National was an A-Level trip. You watched a disturbing play, in which hundreds of rabbits were killed, and even though it wasn't real you cried and began panicking and your best friend held your hand.

> *Walked to Westminster Bridge — got involved in fete/carnival*
> *celebrating 'Walk World' — went into tents — watched open-air*
> *bands — played on bouncy objects — got iced lolly and ate it*
> *walking over bridge towards Big Ben and Parliament*

How many miles must you have walked that day? This scrappy chattering four-year-old and her white-haired guide. A check on the map puts it at about nine miles.

It seems inconceivable now. Nine miles. You can only picture her how she was, the last time you saw her. Immobile, breathless, the oxygen machine. But she never learned to drive, she had always been a walker. Just like your mother was, you were, still are. You and your children think nothing of a ten-mile romp. Adventure. Without the Post-its. Following your nose.

What will happen when you can't walk any more? It seems impossible, as it must have done then to her.

> *Up Whitehall — noted Westminster Abbey — mounted*
> *guardsmen outside St James's Palace — Mrs Thatcher's House*

'Mrs Thatcher'. Yes. You never agreed on politics. She once said the reason why her dog had one short red lead tied on to one long blue lead was because she was mainly Conservative, but Labour also had a point.

You were raised with your political eyes open. Taken on anti-Thatcher marches in your pram. There were postcards of leftie slogans and feminist satire cartoons on your fridge. It took a long time to realise how poor you were, because it was always drilled into you how other people were much worse off.

When you were five, you put your dried fruit treats into envelopes and scrawled AFRICA and INDIA on them for the post. Seven, and you were a passionate member of the Vegetarian Society, whose photocopied zine came monthly through the door, with horrific images of cows being slaughtered, and posters saying DYING TO MEAT YOU, which you put on your bedroom wall. Nine, and you wrote to John Major about animal cruelty in the meat industry. You got a letter on Downing Street paper back. Around the same time, Linda McCartney launched her vegetarian food range and you thought you had done that, you'd made that happen somehow.

Your gran cooked your brother meat sausages, and delighted in being as controversial and offensive as she could.

Trafalgar Square – Nelson – Lions mainly covered (being cleaned) – Fountains – Playing – Pigeons

Trafalgar Square. How many times did you cry there? Usually in the middle of the night, after your shift at a grotty club. Waiting for night buses. Once you were assaulted. Once, in deepest winter, you saw a woman with a tiny baby begging on the street. You had some birthday money in your pocket, you were on your way home from visiting your gran. You went into a 24-hour newsagents and spent it all on nappies, formula, food. You went out to give them the abundance. But the mother and baby had gone.

> *Eaten non-stop all day – took bridge rolls with luncheon meat and cheese portions and wotsits – garibaldi biscuits – jelly bears – drink – Holly had tub of strawberry angel delight – got cake and drink at National Theatre – iced lollies – cheese sandwiches on train coming home*

Ate 'non-stop all day'. Yes, your gran was synonymous with food. When she was a child, her parents ran a corner shop. The excitement – they were going to start selling real Italian ice cream. A huge wooden model arrived, to advertise it. But then Europe erupted, and the ice cream never came. She spent the war playing with the model with her friends, climbing on it, licking it, imagining how ice cream might taste.

You don't have to eat the ice cream to taste the ice cream.

A mantra that sums her up. You don't have to be born in the sixteenth century to be a Tudor. You don't have to have money to know the riches of the world. You don't have to publish a book to be a writer. You don't have to remember London when you were four to be right there.

This was her legacy. This was what she taught you. To hold real life lightly and imaginative life tight. Truth is a fusion of fact and fabrication. Stories are what matter. The stories you leave behind.

Imagination is powerful magic. The greatest source of freedom in the world. But when your own mother was a child, your gran's wand was broken. Imagination a luxury when you're trapped on the edge. When you're clutching onto life with white knuckles, as she had been when your mother was young. When you're raising small children with no money, keeping up appearances when your husband's in the asylum, before the divorce.

But with you, her wand was infinite, and she sent you sparkling and sure into the world. For her, you were a canvas onto which she painted the life she'd craved. Your portrait became her self-portrait. One she could finally be proud to hang on a wall.

As they all said later, you got the best of her. And they were happy for you. No edge. You got the best of her. Trips, treats, cuddles. Knowledge, stories, games. But you're painfully aware now of the exclusivity of your us-ness. What you received from her as a grandmother was not what her own children received. To see yourself as your child sees you is terrifying. To see yourself in your grandchild's eyes is safer somehow.

You frame the Post-its and show them to your children. They were young when she died, but still remember her well.

Like you, they too have her Post-its. How many she must have gone through in her life – stuck onto newspaper articles she'd cut out for you, or on a seed packet with planting advice. Explaining a random jumble-sale find. Adding a footnote to the main letter she'd forgot. The little carved nativity set you get out each Christmas still has her Post-it note explaining where and when she bought it and why. The handbag you inherited, that once belonged to her mother, also has a Post-it note of origin tucked inside.

Your sons ask what Erythroped A is – the brand of antibiotics emblazoned on the notes.

> GG ran a doctor's surgery, you explain to them. She got a lifetime's supply of free stationery from medical reps with the names of different medicines on.

> Didn't she also get our treasure pots from the doctors?

He's talking about the urine-sample jars she spent thirty years sneaking home – first to store and label your own little treasure collections, then to make reliquaries of theirs. She had always been light-fingered (or we might say resourceful). She helped herself to cuttings from posh gardens she visited, making her own garden a scrapbook of blooms. Grapes from the supermarket (*Just a little tester*). Hovering at sample stalls, cheese cubes on little sticks. Running jumble sales in her village so she would be there early and take what she wanted before the punters came in.

From the surgery – along with urine pots, first-aid bits, enough plasters to dress three generations of wounds, and rolls of cotton wool thicker than your arm to make Christmas decoration snow – she mainly got stationery, branded Amarox Ltd, Ennogen Healthcare, Merck Sharp & Dohme, on which she wrote count-less letters, certainly hundreds of thousands, sent to every corner of the globe. We joked that she kept the post going. For her birthdays, you bought her envelopes and stamps. She started writing Christmas cards in October, receiving hundreds in December in return.

Distance across place was like distance across centuries – give her enough and she could fill in the rest.

You are grateful, almost, for the moves that brought you distance – to Cornwall, South Africa, London, Sussex, France. Otherwise you – and now your children – wouldn't have this hoard of her handwriting, keeping her alive still, in suitcases, boxes, folders, drawers. There were phone calls and meet-ups of course, but she knew they'd be ephemeral while letters lived on. She was writing the present for the future, when she'd be long dead and the present would be past.

As you hang the Post-its, you wonder why she wrote them. She didn't keep them, so it wasn't for her. She wrote about you in the third person, so it wasn't for you either. And there was something more than her compulsive posterity in them somehow. As you stand back and look at them (wonky of course, everything is), one line, the final line, stands out bigger than the rest:

SHE HAD LABEL IN HER POCKET

And then – it all makes sense to you. Suddenly, another person joins you and your gran on the wall.

The label in your pocket would have contained your mum's information. When your gran wrote these Post-its, she was bringing along your mum.

She wrote these Post-its to help your mum imagine herself into the day afterwards – everything we did, saw, spoke about, ate. But she also wrote them to say: *You can trust me with your daughter. I looked after her, and she was happy. It was all okay.*

You were so little – not even at school yet. Maybe it was your first proper day so far from home without your mum. Maybe it was a cause of great anxiety. Maybe your mum had been dreading it. Maybe your gran insisted, and your mum had to trust, let go.

The white spaces on the mount between the Post-its hold a whole other story now. One you couldn't have realised till you became a mother yourself. When your eldest was eight, your mum took him alone on an adventure. A week in Wales, a rite of passage, the umbilical cord pulled tight. But she took you with them, in messages, photographs, updates and FaceTimes. Your mother was telling you, as her mother had been telling her: *You can trust me with your son. I've got this. You are always here with him, wherever we go.*

Your mother treads so gently on your own motherhood. She takes such care to sanctify your place between herself and your sons. They love her more than anyone, but she would never come between you. And you see now that, in many ways, your own gran did. The closeness you and your gran shared left no space for anyone else. She sought ways to be deliberately different from your mother, to provocatively undermine or overrule her daughter's mothering to gain your love. To seal it and celebrate it as something separate, just the two of you.

When you had children, your mum chose a different kind of grandmothering – one made not of lines and closed shapes but dots, all of you dots, with soft threads weaving around each other, fluid and welcoming, the connection spacious, safe and strong.

Now you are a mother, you understand your own mother. Your children might have children, and understand something about you. And when you are a grandmother, you'll understand your own gran differently.

This constant procession of becoming and unbecoming. From each to each, a legacy. Something to learn.

What is this legacy? To own our loving.

What is the learning? To love, but not own.

Cousin John

There's a family tree in your grandmother's handwriting – five pages and two centuries of people, held together by genetics and old tape. You know the faces of fifteen of the names, a couple more you could pick out from photos. Beyond that, a scattering of stories: a wedding, a war death, a stillborn son. Your gran knew all the lines' secrets. The ones she didn't know she made up.

It's interesting, then, to see what she omitted. Like when she let slip about Cousin John.

I don't like the Japanese, she'd said, when you told her you were planning a trip to Japan. The usual reasons she gave about certain countries: *They don't play cricket. They don't use knives and forks.*

But then, like a footnote – which, now she's gone, will remain so – she added: *And of course there was Cousin John.*

You were going to Japan to see your best friend. Your only friend, really, if truth be told. Half Japanese, he exploded technicolour on your childhood and ignited a spark in you to live, live, live.

You wrote songs together and choreographed dance routines. The first time you had in-jokes and intimacy with a friend. At night when his mum (how you loved her, tall like a willow tree, her beautiful clothes, her chocolate cake) went to bed, you watched *Queer As Folk* on video with the sound turned down.

When he went to Japan in school holidays, he brought things back like he'd been to a different planet. Technology you couldn't believe, and stationery with kanji speech-bubbles from cute cartoon animals' mouths, and a street-fashion magazine called *Fruits* that became your bible for how to dress.

Suddenly non-uniform days were your territory. He made you feel like you didn't have to hide. He opened the skin that had always restricted you and out you burst, bold and bright. Skirts over skirts, clashing colours, weird materials, pencils in tiny buns all over your head, chunky jewellery you made from the bead shop, patterned tights with chunky sandals, a headband with Playmobil people glue-gunned on.

When he moved back to Japan you were devastated. How could you survive this grey world alone.

You saved up waitressing wages to visit him. You were sixteen years old, and had never been on a plane. Your gran, who had been twice to America, took the matter in her practical hands: A map of the airport. What happens when. What people will ask for along the way. What happens to your suitcase when it disappears down the conveyor. Useful things for your on-plane

237

bag. How to use the plane toilet. The food that comes in little trays.

You relied on her instructions to get onto the plane. But from then, you were on your own — and thirsty. You didn't know you had to press a button to request water. You arrived in Tokyo, parched and confused. Everyone wore facemasks. You couldn't find your friend. You were bamboozled by the airport toilets. So many buttons. So you held it in.

People, so many people. Half a million in Cornwall. Thirteen million in Tokyo alone.

People, and lights, and buildings, and videos playing on towering screens. Streets and more streets, shops and more shops, and everywhere clean, so clean. The train so fast, your friend's finger on the metro map, trying to explain the stops.

You're looking at the map, and you're looking at your friend, and you're looking all around you, and you're drinking it all in, tuning into chatter that is going on around you in this soft strange staccato tongue — you're asking him about the face masks, about his new school, his boyfriend, his mum — you're holding his hand, he's holding yours and your luggage, taking you on and off these trains —you stop talking sometimes and just burst out laughing, looking at each other, looking at your best friend, different now but still your best friend, you're sure of it — and it's marvellous, oh it's marvellous, just to be here, impossible to be here, a girl like you.

You slept on the floor of the small neat bedroom next to the bunkbeds your friend and his older brother shared, and you stayed up late talking about sex, of which you knew nothing, and whether his brother would get engaged or not, because in Japan, girls expected to marry young – and then in the morning, or was it the night still, there was an earthquake, and books fell onto your head.

Your friend still had a week of school left, so you were free to roam Tokyo alone. You had a map, and a guidebook, and he wrote you instructions, and put a note in your pocket with his number and address. On the first day, you came out the wrong side of the station and panicked. You showed the note to someone and they drew a map of the way.

After that, he taught you how to ask questions beginning 'Where is' – but as soon as you asked a stranger you realised you could not decipher their replies. You got lost, and you couldn't follow your nose because the city was immaculate and nothing smelled.

You found your bearings, bought cute stationary, wrote letters. Found a place to buy apples because you were scared of the food.

Your best friend dazzled you. He was king of this land. So stylish, so popular, so connected. He strutted and partied and laughed. How had Cornwall ever been enough to contain him. You felt parochial and childish. Ashamed. He had grown up, grown outward. You'd grown inward. His world, vast. Yours, small.

You watched a TV show when you were there, in which a woman contorted herself into impossible places – a suitcase in an airport, a washing machine in a laundrette – then burst out to surprise people. Everybody laughed.

You could also contort yourself into small places. But you never wanted to come out.

We grow to the size of the world around us. You remember seeing once, in a museum, a dead toad locked in a hollow in a stone. It had crawled in there as a baby and grown until it couldn't get out. That's why we must find homes for ourselves beyond four walls.

You got drunk for the first time in Tokyo, on drinks you couldn't name. You went to the nightclub where his brother worked and watched sailors in white uniforms with handheld camcorders videoing girls. They were women of course, but there was a schoolgirl fashion trend, so they appeared coy and virginal in their tucked-up white shirts.

You watched the men watching the women through their cameras, and when you had drunk too much you watched yourself watching them watching them.

It was cherry blossom time. The trees were dazzling with pink precision. You paid to have a picnic in a sacred park. You sent a postcard of the pink trees to your grandmother. You wrote her many letters during your three weeks in Japan, trying to convey the awe of the place, the people. How desperately you wanted to show her cutlery and cricket didn't matter after all.

She knew so much, but you were beginning to realise she had limits. That there were topics to which her door remained firmly closed. That behind the doors were locked-up mysteries and she wouldn't let anyone in.

Sometimes you caught glimpses of the woman your mother knew: stubborn, closed-minded, prejudiced, sharp-tongued, unable or unwilling to emotionally process the great many wrongs she'd endured. Your mum, now a therapist, opening the heart-door to healing. Your gran, petty and petulant, slamming it in her face.

You didn't want to experience this side of her. You got the best of her – everyone said. So much of your world had been built on her safe foundations. But what if you couldn't always trust her bricks?

Twenty years later, you're sitting in your garden, when the 'Last Post' comes to you from the village over the fields. Strange – August, not November. No pinned-on poppies, no bunting in the street. You check the news: V-J Day. The bugle grieves in arpeggios. A minute's silence – which you observe – then the church bells toll.

And of course there was Cousin John.

You'd forgotten all about that conversation. It hadn't seemed important to you back then. You were sixteen, and living in the present. You were used to your gran's stories, sometimes true, often not.

You don't actually remember if he was a cousin. You don't even know if he was John. You consult her family tree, but there's no information.

You message the family – *Does anyone remember what relative was a prisoner of war in Japan?*

Blanks. No one's heard that story. Your gran was a library from which you'd all borrowed different books.

She's gone. There's no one to ask about it. So, as she'd have done, you will have to make it up.

And so – you imagine John, as that's what we'll call him, to have been a quiet man. The men you imagine often are.

A quiet man, in his early twenties, seventy-five years ago on V-J Day. A skeleton man, with blank socket eyes, trying to hold on to what's left of his bones, as the men around him rabble and riot, hurling themselves against the prison hut door. One last push of strength from the strengthless, shouting We're here! to the Americans outside.

But let's not put the quiet man with them. Let's put him crouching in the corner of the room. Let's have him shushing out the jangle of liberation that clanked like metal all around.

Let's have the Americans almost leave without him, because he made himself so small they miss him there. And when they find him, they have to hold him like a child and carry him to the Humvee as he says, No, please no.

The quiet man was fated for a quiet life. To work his way up from carpenter's apprentice to become a joiner for a local firm, enough to buy a two-up two-down in the small market town he grew up in, with a wife he likes enough, and a boy and a girl. A potato patch, a well-organised tool shed, tea with two sugars, and hutched rabbits for the pot. A week away a year to Hunstanton, and Christmas at his mother's, who complains his wife does the turkey all wrong.

But no – nineteen, holding a gun in Malaya. Impossible, just impossible, a boy like him here. Forced to his knees when Singapore falls. He goes with them quietly. Not a time to start shouting. Keep your head down and your nose clean lad, his dad always said.

He makes himself a spot, in the metal hut he's herded into, between the shit-stained wall and the bucket latrine. Stays small enough and quiet enough for his hutmates not to bother him, even when they try – and fail, no guts left – to shit. Does what he's told, when he's told it. Keeps on going when the others drop and die.

In his mind, he plays a long game of snooker. This is where he goes, inside. Counting the balls, listing the colours. Picturing them on the baize. Rubbing the chalk on his cue. Lining up shots he never takes.

So when the doors burst in, on the fifteenth of August, and his hutmates riot, and the Yankee Doodles yell, he stays crouched in the corner screaming, No! No! No! – only of course he is silent, no words come out.

They get out quickly. He's left there alone. He remembers the murder last winter – a fight over rice, the guy was new. Everyone dragged out by guards, except the quiet man, hiding in the corner, latrine bucket on his head. Quiet and alone for a moment, his mind playing snooker, as his hutmates were shot.

He closes his eyes. The sound of the Americans fades into the distance. Maybe he can just die his quiet death here now. But a bright flash burns his eyes open, and he moves, and a photographer calls out: Hey! One still here!

The snapper takes the quiet man's photograph. Tomorrow, it will appear all over the world.

The quiet man flies home in a roaring tin can with rabbling comrades, whose bones shunt into his bones, as they eat, drink, talk, puke, cough, scratch, sing. Impossible, imagine it, impossible. Impossible for him to be here, a man like him.

To force a quiet man into liberation is to ask of that quiet man too much. He doesn't want to be a part of world history. Keep your liberation, there is nothing here to save. When the plane lands and he refuses to leave it, he is saying:

I have worked too hard to shrink this existence, and I am not ready, and you are all too loud.

You still chat now and then with your best friend from childhood. He is an artist now, quite famous, in Berlin. You go to see him, in that city full of war ghosts. People perched with picnics on the Holocaust memorial. A parking lot built over where Hitler supposedly died.

You're three months pregnant, second child. So it's lunch with your friend, not a glamorous night out. It's hot. You order iced cordial. You put a shoebox on the table between your plates.

I can't believe you kept all this! he says.

The box contains all your relics from Japan. All your photos, the teenage letters you'd exchanged, your tatty maps and ticket stubs, souvenir chopsticks, the wrapper from a blueberry chocolate bar you liked, the Japanese pop mixtapes he made you and you listened to on repeat. Your gran's guide to airports. Your precious *Fruits* fashion magazine. His mother's chocolate-cake recipe. The Playmobil-people crown.

You come from women who can't throw anything away.

Externalise the spectres and you exorcise your bones.

You came back from Japan entirely different. You had bought suede boots with a platform almost a foot tall. Your mum worried you'd break your neck on them but what you broke was the boundary between your child self and the world.

There was one thing you and Cousin John had in common: you both went to Japan and both came back changed. Later you'd both attempt suicide, but only one of you would succeed.

A lot of them did, of course, your grandmother had said.

Perhaps that's why no one told his story. And why you are now having to make it up.

It's easier to make imaginary men quiet. Else you have to think of the noisy ones you're trying to forget. That recurring motif in the family tree: quiet girl, loud man.

The Japanese for quiet is *shizukana*. Our two tongues share the *shhh*. There's a separate word for silence: *chinmoku*. The route to enlightenment, an art. The only language to have a word that means 'room in complete silence'. In English, the word 'awkward' might be used.

You remember now how quiet the quiet places were. The temples, the gardens, the orange groves. Meditative, respectful. Even the plane was so quiet. The recognition that our voices take up as much space as flesh.

There's a Japanese saying: *Let silence talk and let language be silent*.

Later, when difficult things leave you utterly voiceless, you'll find comfort in a Quaker meeting-house hall. You'll walk in by accident one Sunday, as if drawn there. A simple room. A hundred or so people, in a square. Then an hour, a whole hour, of silence. You will close your eyes. You will wrestle the discomfort. When you open them again, you see, for a moment, your child-self skipping, in a long white dress with red ribbons in her hair. You will cry profusely in that silence, but you won't be able to articulate why.

In her final years, your gran will open the door to your mother. They'll speak every Sunday for hours. Your mum will use the family tree as a transitional object, to ignite conversations and heal wounds. Your mum is interested in epigenetics. She is tracing the patterns of inheritance handed down. Through telling the stories of others, your gran inadvertently tells the story of herself. The true story, the cellular story, the psychologist's story, of who she is and why she is and how she is.

There are kinds of silences that protect you. But there are kinds that do you harm. So you write. You write quietly, of loud things. You take up space, without speaking a word.

Where Have You Gone

The last time you spoke to your grandmother, you had your first and only row. Two things had happened that you'd never expected: you'd become a mother, and she'd become old.

You'd taken the children, still young then, to visit her. You were in Sainsbury's, the toddler acting up. Your gran in a wheelchair, pushed by your auntie-mum. You got to the tills, and she suddenly snapped. The meagre air left in those lungs of hers surged out a sharpness that smote like a smack. A comment about your bad mothering. You thought, if she'd had strength enough, she'd have given you a slap.

You fled. Took the children. Marched back to your auntie-mum's house. The children confused. You seething. Ashamed.

That wasn't your grandmother. Where had she gone.

Let time take care of it, you thought, like all cowards. It seemed impossible there wouldn't be time left.

Your gran often talked about writing her memoirs. She even had a title: '*A Bucketful of Plums*'.

When she'd left the Viking estate to rent a cottage, a neighbour had welcomed her with a bucket of plums that must have become, for your gran, a symbol of shedding her old selves and starting anew. To arrive in a place where no one knew what she'd been through. To be seen as educated, cultured, knowledgeable. Well-spoken, well-mannered, well-groomed. She was happy in that new version of herself, in that cottage. She was Somebody. An indispensable part of village life. Important, loved and admired. Stories selected and edited to create a narrative which finally reflected a life she could live.

What would she have written in her memoir? None of the bad stuff, you're sure about that. Her unlived life — not her lived life. The stories of others. The illuminated past. She'd have taken the skeleton of the family tree in winter and painted her own bright fecund foliage on.
A themoir, not memoir. Half invented. All true.

If writing is the act of truth-telling, imagining, and editing, then your gran wrote more than anyone, without publishing a word.

But that sharp tongue at the supermarket was raw and unfiltered, from a place in your grandmother that you didn't know. A cut before rupture. You had never seen her cross.

Where did it begin, that rupture? Perhaps with the phone call a few years before.

> They've found something on my lungs. Nothing to worry about.
>
> Really?
>
> Really, treasure. I'm fine. Just wanted to let you know.

You remember that phone call, standing in your sons' small shared bedroom. The youngest, not yet two, had only just moved in here from your bed. The usual opener – Gran, it's expensive to call a mobile, hang up and I'll call you straight back.

She never learnt to use a mobile. She always preferred letters. Now you're glad. It meant your children knew the excitement of her parcels, arriving weekly full of books, little toys, pocket money, sweets. Knew her handwriting on the envelope, on her letters, on the Post-it notes with addendums, explanations of things.

She knew them so well. Knew the eldest shared her love of historical knowledge, despite only being four, sending him her old history magazines, or articles from newspapers, or guidebooks from castles and museums. She knew the youngest loved everything cute and cuddly, sending him little drawings of rabbits or cats she had done.

Sometimes she would send them things of hers, things that were important, objects that meant little to them now but would mean much to them later on. Increasingly – although you dismissed it – she wrote as if she were mortal. Which of course she wasn't. She'd live forever. She was your gran.

> I'll come up for Christmas, you told her. With the boys.

But in the end, for whatever reason, you didn't go. Then –

> I'll come up for your birthday.

A year passed. You still didn't visit.

If you went, you'd have to face her mortality. You'd spent so long making things up together that reality was far too hard. The updates from your auntie, too much for you. An oxygen machine, although she didn't always need it. A wheelchair for their Saturday mooch. Tiredness. On the phone, she gets breathless. She'll have to move into a home.

Your auntie sends a photo of her looking happy.

Where has she gone. Get those tubes out her nose.

Finally you did go. There was the sharp tongue at the supermarket.

You didn't speak to her or see her again.

On the day of the international Women's March, you wrote to her. It felt fitting. You'd been marching all your lives. Endured combat with men with clear faces, hand to hand, eye to eye, only to discover that advancing behind them were row upon row of more faceless troops. For women, there will always be battles. The war will never be won.

Your gran was the flag-bearer, first woman, origin woman. The matriarch. Boudicca in a cottage, you joked.

You knew somehow it would be the last letter you wrote her. It went on and on, as you avoided the end. Everything she meant to you. What you'd shared, who you'd been together. An apology. Too late. Overdue.

You got the best of her, everybody said that. So much of what you are now is because of her. Could a grandmother and grand-daughter have been closer? You *were* each other. So much of you the same.

You sent her the letter for her birthday. Eight days later, she was gone.

The funeral parlour had a viewing room. Flowers. Low light. Velvet drapes. The door was half open. Your grandmother inside. But you ran back upstairs again. You couldn't go in.

How long did you spend avoiding that room of hers? Long enough to hear the same piece of harp music on repeat. Running up the stairs, then creeping back down them, then running up again, the red carpet patterned with white fleur-de-lis. The same carpet continuing into the room. You know this because you stared at it, not looking up.

You walked in backwards, and turned to the wall, and said out loud to her –

Where have you gone?

Repeating that question, inching around the walls with your back to her, too scared to look. You dared one glance. Enough to see how tiny she was, like death had peeled her layers back to her girl-self. She wasn't there. Why couldn't you sing to her. Sing *non nobis domine*. Lean in close. Kiss her head.

Where have you gone?

It seems macabre, but you took a picture. Closed your eyes and pointed your phone. In case one day, you'd be ready to look at her. In the future, when the present became past.

When all of you sang at her funeral – the church so packed that some had to stand – the sound was incredible, so loud, so much strength in it, holy and joyously loud, and you pushed your way through it, through the waves of this hymning, to the lectern at the front, with your notes.

Your eulogy raised her out of her coffin. People cried and laughed. Afterwards, they asked for a copy. *I hope someone will write a eulogy like that for me*, one said. Because isn't that what we all want – to leave behind stories that say. This is me. This is who I tried to be. Who I was.

We tell stories to invent and reinvent ourselves. To makes sense of the nonsensical. Impose order on the mess. To begin again, become again, become Other. To patchwork the gap between who we shouldwouldcould have been and who we reluctantly, impossibly, became.

We write, because we are nothing but thin skins and fragilities, and stories make solid what would otherwise break.

We write to say: Here – forge these bones of mine with your bones and together we'll be strong enough to survive this world. And when this world's over, we'll live on in that feeling, in the connection of these stories between my bones and your bones.

Where have you gone?

You realise you are lucky that only death brought that question. How present you'd been together, all your lives. *We're the same, you and me.* She always said that. So where have *we* gone? Where are *we* now?

You're surprised, in old photos, how slim she was. All lines and angles and cinched Sixties waist. She was thin as a mother, but vast as a grandmother, her body and her lovingness expanding hand in hand.

You took her body so completely for granted. You never even noticed it. She was all mind to you. Geographical distance limited physical closeness. She was ink on letters, a voice on the phone.

What was her own relationship with her body? Pragmatic and matter-of-fact – from her years on the desk in the doctor's surgery, and her Christian belief that she was merely 'passing through'. Her body was a vessel. From the earth, to the earth. No pretence, no squeamishness, no ego, sensuality, or pride.

And yet – she was always in layers. You never saw her unclothed. She never went swimming. Apart from her face and hands, you never saw her skin.

How much had she felt the disappointment of her female body? The daughter who should have been a son. The intelligent young woman who should have been a graduate. How that body betrayed her. Interrupted her becoming. Bowed to its feminine prerogative, conceiving and birthing with ease.

A female body that buckled under the might of male violence. Curtsied to authority. Bullied for years by her boss.

Yet, this was her old self. The woman in those photographs. The one you heard about, not the one you knew.

The woman you saw was male and female. Invulnerable, inde-pendent, outspoken, strong. An ability to shock, crack jokes, be controversial. Logical and rational. Two fingers, behind her back, up to the world. Perhaps – as you have read in science journals – cells of her lost brother grew into her, in utero, becoming part of her inside.

Perhaps she was shaped by the fierce empowerment of her two daughters. She may have dismissed the dogma of feminist politics, but she witnessed what it took, the fight it took, for them to be strong. She was so proud of them. But, for her, they were also mirrors. Her story and their story, hard to separate. Her part, difficult to recognise, face up to, brought her pain.

And then there was you. A blank canvas. A chance to begin again. To be the person she wanted to be, when as a mother she'd had no choice.

What was she trying to instil in you, when you were little more than a toddler, standing at the boating lake reciting the speech of Elizabeth 1?

> *I may have the body of a weak and feeble woman but I have the heart and the stomach of a king!*

Was it a warning?

> *These female bodies of ours are powerless but make your mind strong and you will crush any man.*

At the end, she was so small. A bag of ashes in your hand. You had filed out the crem to the Ashes test match theme tune – 'Soul Limbo'. She had always liked a joke.

It took two years to do something with that part of her. February; the anniversary; Imbolc. You and mother walk the steep track one bright morning, looking for a spot on the Downs.

You carry a box of snowdrops, sealed against the wind, clutching it tight, so aware of its fragility that someone stops and asks if there's an animal inside.

You scout for a spot, as if divining for it. As if a burst of gold light would suddenly reveal the way. You settle on a thicket of wind-bent hawthorns, bowing over the fields and paths that lead back to your home.

Your gran had never been to the village you'd moved to after she was gone. But she would have loved it, the similarity to her own. She would have liked to think of herself up there, an earthy guardian, keeping watch over you and your home.

Your mother digs a hole in a cleave in the tree roots. Enough to bury a photograph and a lock of white hair. You slip the earth back delicately together, your hands, your mother's hands, the snowdrops on top. The sunlight. No words. Sharing presence.

There are snail shells, empty, around the tree roots. You both get the idea, unspoken, at the same time. You stand at the edge, where green grass becomes chalk slope. You lob the snail shells as far as you can.

Snails for Jesus! you cry, half-laughing, enacting her garden routine from when you were young.

Did you throw the ashes too?

You should remember. But you don't.

Where have you gone?

You're still asking that question. It's been five years now. You could do with her help. The ache of her absence gets deeper. There was so much more to share. What phone calls you could be having – about the children, the village, gardening, the dog, the chickens, her reading, your work.

One day, when things are particularly difficult, you pick a poetry book randomly off the shelf. A postcard slips out. Her hand-writing, from almost twenty years ago, saying everything you need to hear now:

> *Glad your garden is looking good. It is such a good therapy. You don't say much about how you are. Lots of mind juggling no doubt. Do you think more about teaching or will it be writing? You are so creative I'd favour the latter for you. I know bills have to be paid but don't sell yourself short.*

Seven years pass. Still no gravestone. Still you all struggle to accept she is gone. Still your children go quiet if they find a reminder. Sometimes the youngest still cries. You still cry, often. You all do. If only you shared her belief in the afterlife and could imagine her as God's head gardener, chucking snails out of Eden.

A space is approved for a headstone, finally, in her village church-yard. You discuss the wording. You don't mind what goes on it. You've made your headstone of sorts.

But when she is laid to rest, you will at last sing to her, *non nobis domine*, and leave snowdrops at her feet.

the most beautiful sounds
I ever heard

my best friend's voice down the phone from a warzone
love you dickhead don't die   love you too

the mute hen a year after rescue who grew all her feathers back
and finally said cluck

the heartbeat on the midwife's monitor after falling belly-hard
and eight months pregnant in the snow

our elderly cat who purrs easy as breathing soft and asleep on
my insomniac chest

hello poddle   hello treasure
i'd give anything to hear that again

the clink of the coin in the phonebox when the first boy i fancied
picked up the phone

when a word i've been struggling to recall returns to me and i
say it like a victory out loud

mum   i'm here darling right here

a dream of a daughter
i'm dora   i know

water wild quiet waves rivers the rush around the rocks in our
cornish secret spot where the freshest redgold water tumbles
round us to the sea

nightingales breaking the moonlight as we lay under blankets
holding hands amongst the trees

look!
meteors peregrines a bone a barn owl whale fins Jupiter toads

the examiner saying i'd passed my driving test and at the age
of thirty-two i was finally free

you're beautiful you're beautiful
though you never believe it

piano keys connecting to my body aged three ten thirty toes
legs soul eyes

quickening breath in his flat with the balcony that felt like paris
when the sun poured in

when you're holding your breath at the end of your overdraft
and the till approves your payment for emergency tampons and
bread

a japanese garden the breeze through the cherry trees the trickle
of tea into porcelain cups

snails for jesus

pages turning in a library

non nobis domine sung by the stove

when my father sang anything in a minor key especially 'annie's song' or 'almaz' and for as long as he was singing he had a heart and it was beautiful and everything would be okay

bike wheels spinning through may sunshine downhill eyes closed hands off *wheeee*

a match struck in france in a power cut the flutter of soft moth wings the hiss of the wick

rustling as the dog bursts out a hedgerow hours after escaping ten miles from home

come on let's swim
strip to knickers not caring the clear river silty and sultry and warm

pounding drums and banger cracks at bonfire thrill fear samba cider rumbling carts of tar

my mother's laugh my auntie's laugh my brother's laugh safe and warm and playing the *i love you as much as* game

a bee swarm caught with my eleven year old gently tipped into a skep back humming in our hive

my mother's whisk whipping the meringue peaks for baked alaska on friday nights when the rain stops one spring evening and in the stillness you can hear the water sucking into the earth like a teenage kiss

toddlers finding peace together giggling giving each other bubble mohawk hairstyles in the bath

skylarks on the downs when i needed to hear them

mummy i love cheese scones but i love you more than all the cheese scones in the world

pens scribbling in a silent classroom

my dead friend's ocarina

hedgehogs twilight snuffle unseen

bright pink sky dawn chorus as my nephew was born into the world in july

end of lockdown first live music bach cello suites my youngest clinging to me as we cried and there was light

spades in soil digging up our potatoes the sizzle of them baking the *mmmmm*

son in the woods in his dinosaur overalls singing to himself *autumn leaves are falling down* slowly spinning under oaks

my music box the spinning ballerina lifting the lid the little tinkling of 'swan lake'

lovers calling me by my surname

laughter unexpected at a funeral when a eulogy brings the dead
briefly joyously back to life

arcade fire glastonbury downpour crowd singing 'wake up' like
a choir at the end of the world

he's alive she's alive   we're alive
the relief after a moment of cheating death

it's going to be okay
it's going to be okay
anytime anyone says it's going to be okay

Inventory of Wonderment

You are eight and ten, and just making sense of things, when the world turns upside down.

Temporary, at first. A thrill to us, almost: no early mornings, no schedules, no school. Then novelty becomes normal, the precarity permanent, the crisis chronic, and your little lives change.

How your young brains, so molten, accept it. I try to adapt, as you do, but it hurts. You flow in the present, see no ripples beyond this. Time is still infinite and circular to you. You still feel immortal. I'm convinced we'll all perish. And if we survive, there'll be grief all the same.

You miss what is missing – the real, the tangible – our family, the library, the swimming pool, your friends. But I grieve for things that you don't know exist yet. I grieve for the people you were supposed to be. All your beautiful becoming, interrupted. Your world shrunk so small, when it should be so vast. I see the consequences of how this will change you – losing yourselves, before you've barely begun.

We three rely on the roots of outsideness. We are all of us happiest on adventures outdoors, exploring ourselves as we explore all around us, finding ourselves in mud, rock, birds, rivers, trees. Without that now, I need to find a new way to weave your fragile little threads into the anchoring tapestry of this world.

Life has shrunk – so let's become microscopic. Discover the vastness inside us instead. Small children need big magic. So we list the inventory of wonderment in our bones.

We work out that, so far, of the ten years we've had together, we've spent 29,200 hours asleep. Cots and bunkbeds and hospital beds, car seats, sofas, tents and dens. Night feeds and nightmares and fevers. Sleep-walking, sleep-talking, dreams. Nights with you on me, over me, each side of me, sprawling and tangling our limbs. When you were babies, I made you both blankets. You still have them now, on your beds. I know I say this so often you mock me, but when we all sleep on the sofa on Friday movie nights, it is my happiest place in the world.

Moons, then. Moons for that sleeping. We calculate that 144 of them have been full. The ones I held your baby-hands in mine to wave goodnight to. The special ones that called us to step into the night.

I wonder if, later, you'll remember the pink moon. Three months into lockdown – a sliver, an arc. Right there, at the front door of our first house, above the plum tree I crashed into when I was learning to drive.

I said, I've never seen a pink moon before!

How is it made? one of you asked.

And the other of you, toothbrush wedged in your molars, told us –

It's the sunset colliding with the night.

We were outside, waiting to clap for the NHS. The church clock struck eight. Whoops erupted all around. Drums banged, spoons clanked on saucepans, car horns beeped over the fields from the road, the church bells ringing – and you, under a pink moon, in your pyjamas, taking your place in this cacophony of sound. How you got swept up in it, clapping, clapping, clapping, your faces like bonfire night, elated, confused.

We clapped, and I didn't want us to stop clapping, because there was belonging and we were not alone. Beginnings and endings. The two of you and me. The bigness of this moment, the small-ness of you.

I watched you and thought: this is something you'll remember. This moment that we're living in is history made flesh. How we might talk about this later, on the other side, and say, Do you remember when we ran outside and clapped? And the moon was pink? And we had our pyjamas on?

A red moon now. The blood moon. The one that wouldn't come again for a hundred years. We headed out, in a break in the storms, to hunt for it, climbing up into the dark wet vertigo of the Downs. Ducking through tunnels where the trees twisted round on themselves, belting out 'Over the Hills and Far Away' and other songs to stay brave. Past wild ponies and cattle and rabbits, the steep slopes so perilous from all the rain that I stopped to teach you how to make an emergency call from my phone.

At the very top – we made it! – we perched on damp rocks and waited and waited. But there was no moon. The cloud cover was a punchline. In spite of everything, we laughed.

To your delight, I'd brought doughnuts. We squidged the red jam out, and held them up to the sky.

See? I said. We don't need to find a blood moon to see one.

As if writing you a manual of mantras for when I'm gone.

Space camp – do you remember? We camped in the garden, between the chicken coop and Mars. It would be the closest to Earth for seventeen years. Be rude not to say hello.

We walked in the field with the Stellarscope, naming patterns in the sky. Every star vivid and countable, Greek myths unfolding in front of our eyes. You could tell me the story behind every constellation. Vega, Arcturus, Cassiopeia. Jupiter and Saturn hung low over the Downs. The fish tails of Pisces darting diagonal off the red dot of Mars.

What giddiness we shared. It increased us, these christenings. The ungraspable on our tongues. Would the stars mean less if we had no names for them? If one day you forget their names, remember that you don't need taxonomy for awe.

You announced that Mars is 38.6 million miles away. How you summon such facts with such ease. Your excitement that, somewhere, three spacecraft had just been sent hurtling, called Hope, Tianwen and Perseverance, by China, America and the UAE.

We were meant to launch one with Russia, you said. But we didn't make it in time, so now we have to wait twenty-six months.

Was it because of coronavirus or Boris Johnson, your little brother asked, swinging the torch, until you told him to stop swinging it, and he didn't, so I took it instead.

The excitement of the tent, after our night walk. Armfuls of blankets piled inside. Hot water bottles in sleeping bags. You told me to wake you up if I heard a hedgehog rustle by. You slept snuggled and I stayed up freezing. It rained, but then it stopped.

You both talked in your sleep that night.

But would it get rid of it? one of you said.

A window opened into you and shut again, before I had time to see inside.

We slept together under three planets, believing we would wake up a bit more wise.

I hope, when you're older, you'll find comfort in darkness. Let the night sky's wonder ease the dark you feel inside. Right now, one of you wants to be an astronaut. But it's easy, when you're an adult, to turn your back on the night.

Suns now. Suns for my sons. When there was sun, we were always outside.

One solstice, we climbed up the Beacon. It had been a bit of a difficult time. Walked up, with big thoughts and big energies, to make ourselves small in big skies. The sea stretched on one side – we couldn't see France, but the blurry turbines you call ghost ships spinning in the wind farm in the waves, and the huge yellow ferry I kept promising we'd go on when we had enough money for a holiday, although we're still waiting after all these years.

On the other side, land staggered like a theatre set, into the Weald from up here in the Downs, sheep and cattle, wild orchids, remote-control gliders divebombing crows, the fields unfolding like sleeping goddesses into green Ravilious paintbrush waves.

How we oriented ourselves, and recorded our belonging, through finding our home, the church, your school. The town in the distance, and the Iron Age hilltop, where neon-flash paragliders were throwing themselves off, and the sheep paths carved by centuries of bleating, and the hurry of the train in the shadow of the clouds.

How you ran wild and screamed your heads off. Made dens in the thicket. Filled your pockets with chalk. We laid out a blanket your GG had knitted, under the hawthorn called the GG Tree, where me and your nan buried a lock of her hair. You played with your chalk, got ice cream down your school shirts. We talked about solstice, about heaven, death and time, because our we-hood is like that – not a mother and two children, but three minds that can keep up with each other to understand anything, big and small.

We went home again, feeling much better. When you feel low, get seven hundred feet high.

We could try and work out how many books we've read, but the calculator would break. The reading gene is strong. You both read for hours a day. Fact and fantasy and fiction. Rereading favourites till you know them by heart. Whenever I worry about your future, I reassure myself you love reading, so you will always be okay.

Instead, we calculate you've eaten 394,308 meals in your lifetimes, not including party food, baby milk or snacks.

You are peppers by the bucketload, and pizza dough, and hummus, and yoghurt with honeycomb from our hives, and pancakes with eggs from our chickens, and sticky toffee Putin, and potatoes out the ground. Soft, hot bread from our neighbour, and your hands on the pasta machine, turning it round. Elderflower cordial we make to ritualise your birthday. The cupcakes you made yourself and sold for charity on your own little stall. Six hundred and twenty-eight birthday candles. You eat everything but aubergine. You love Japanese food.

And apples. Do you remember all those apples? The long Septembers when we picked and picked. Your animated strategies, how high you climbed, how far you reached. Your glee at getting the one you wanted, the shout of, It's perfect! How carefully you passed them to each other so they wouldn't bruise.

I remember watching you once and feeling so full of love for you. How every apple perfectly fitted your cupped hands. Me at the bottom, scuffing the windfalls, wrapping the good ones you passed me in old pages of the *London Review of Books*, distracted by a poem or an article, as you rattled out apple stories, science and mythology both.

How many? We counted six, seven hundred. The trees unusually generous that year – we kept remarking on it, grateful, amazed – we wondered if it was a gift from our beehives under the boughs. We chopped and cooked, till it felt like we were made of them. Apple compote, apple butter, apple cake, apple crumble, apple pie. Apple juice, made laboriously on the old village apple press. Belly full, freezer full, larder full, and the winter ahead of crates of them, nestling in newspaper in the shed.

Make the most of every gift, my children. Find abundance when all else is in short supply.
Every month, every season, brings gifts to us. Never give up looking for them, and harvesting what you can. Make use of everything you are given. The goodness of you comes from the goodness of the land.

Remember the trees? Hundreds we planted. Your little hands untangling the fragile roots of saplings and tethering them deep into the clod. Sliding in the tree supports. Mulching. Your rosy-cheeked ripples of purpose. The worms you held gently in your little muddy hands.

These trees will be the knots in the handkerchief of your childhood. I imagine you coming back here, forty, sixty years from now, maybe with children, grandchildren, of your own, and standing in the forest we planted with our friends.

Run your hands along the bark. Find the Family Tree we planted – one for us, one for your nan, your cousins, your great-auntie and uncle, a beech tree for GG, a wonky dog-rose for our cross-eyed dog.

We have planted ourselves in this land, my boys. We three, made of mud, bird and bark. I need you to remember this, because when I go, the land will stay with you. You will need to recover our we-hood where you can.

Feel yourselves into each season. Never lose your wonderment to dread.

At some point, adults start dreading the winter. Embrace it. Everything has to sleep. Cherish bright cold days, bright colder nights. Fires and blankets and arctic gales. We were upset the first time the winds destroyed the garden, but we got used to it after that. Hens to bed at four, humans to bed by seven. Potatoes we dug up and ate, chins dripping with hot butter. Chapped lips, hot honey and lemon drinks, skin red raw from the cold. One of you loves hats, scarves and gloves. The other of you won't even wear a coat.

Remember the word we made – *wintumn*. The shift between seasons. Last swallows, first frost. A sun that rose, unexpected, igniting a dormant life-lust within. Deer that scatter as if never there. Meadows full of mushrooms. Webs jewelled with dew. Horses in the mist, and hoards of doomed pheasants (when you're older you will rescue them and run a sanctuary, you say). Hunters in tweed outside the pub smoking breakfast cigarettes (you ask if you can swear at them, and I say, Yes but in your head).

When you are dismayed at the winter, plant whips in hope of spring. Sift through compost and thank the chickens for making black gold. Order logs, and make a human chain down the garden, and play Jenga to stack them up. Gather your own kindling in the summer. You can survive anything when you prepare. Keep buying hot lunches for the woman in the doorway in town with a sign that says God Bless. Remember the winter the pond froze over and you made an ice factory with the girl next door, the dog feasting on the ice.

Do you remember when I asked you to remind me that November is actually nice? If I write it here, maybe you'll remember it is too. Eleven hours of daylight; Leonid meteors; soup and blankets; bonfires miles away scarletting the skies. Lambs in the field, impossibly. At the beginning of the month, we watched newborns die. How the farmer took the steaming bundles and flung them off into the bush, and I said, Don't look. Colds we pass around us, everyone ill, but we keep on going, noticing the colour, the light.

Hold on to light. Please hold on to it. Light is the hopeful way to mark time. It will wax and wane, for a while there won't be enough of it, but after winter solstice we get a whole new minute of it each day, so do something to mark that and make it count. Breathe. Be still. Sooner than you think, the sun won't set till after four. Such a good thing to hold on to. The coming of the light.

Things will be different, so the sun says.

You told me once that when the sun explodes, it will take eight minutes and twenty-three seconds to realise it on Earth.

The biggest number of all – our breaths. We have taken together 300 million between us. How you marvel at such a big number, and make your chests heave in and out quickly to add a few more.

I have been there for all of them. The shallow ones when you were nervous. The deep ones in your sleep. The wheezy ones in hospital. The ones interrupted by hiccups and the ones that stop when you laugh. Panting from running, climbing, swimming. Using our lungs up screaming Traiiiiiiiiiiiiiin when we see one, keeping the sound going and going without taking a breath till it has passed.

Every breath tells your body to keep going. There will be times when you want to give up.
When you're seized by lostness, darkness, aloneness. We all have times when we become a black hole.

When that happens, find something else that's breathing. A dog, a cat, a tree. Latch yourself on to it, and listen to it breathing. Swallow their breath into yours.

Step outside. Be feral when you need to be. Breathe into the land as the land breathes into you. Share that air. Forget ironing shirts. But maybe your nan has a point about a hairbrush now and then.

You tell me we are made of seven billion billion billion atoms. I can feel every one of them as I write this all down. It's a rush to feel that, like falling in love. Remembering is like falling in love with you, with us, again and again.

It is my job to tell you what love is, and when you need to know it most I might not be around.

I need you to know all this now because I can't tell you about it when I'm gone. When the Gone Women go, they take so much with them. You don't need more riddles. You will have enough of your own.

I need you to know all this because one day you will bury me and I need to be more than my bones. I can't take this marrow of mine with me. So it has to be remembered, written down, retold.

You need to remember because one day I won't. And if love is anything it is this: an archive of everything our lives have been together, every sight, smell, sound, every kiss and sob and argument, every moment no matter how small, the certain way the light hit your face when we lay on our backs to hear nightingales, the summer your back burnt into a peelable map, chickenpox, appendix, asthma, puke, every seizure, every meltdown, the favourite jumpers, names of teddies, the lunchbox that melted on the left-on hob, the miles of walking with snacks and songs, Bone Bay and toothbrushes, your butterfly wings.

I have known you far longer than you have known yourselves. My bones have carried this knowingness, my skin, my womb. It is a form of becoming, from I-hood to we-hood – you becoming yourselves, me becoming how you see me. Along the way, I know myself in epiphanies or I do not know myself at all.

Soon, there will be a tipping point when you grow up and leave home and I won't know as much about you any more. My daily knowing, so domestic and tangible, will become an imagined knowing in my mind.

I will take all the facts I have for you and make tiny fictions to remember who you are. Please – give me enough to keep living these. Call me, visit, let's have weekends away. I can make a lot out of very little. Bring me your adulthoods and I will lay them down on your childhoods. Perhaps ageing, old age, is this – the buckling of the body under years of everyone's layers.

We don't know that we need to know our parents, until something happens that compels us to know. A death, perhaps. A dysfunction. A behaviour not understood. A broken heart that makes you wonder about their broken hearts. Experiencing their choices in your choices. Seeing their parenthood in your parenthood. Seeing their strife in yours.

It is empathy, when we open that divide. So here – here is all of me, in these pages. The good, the bad, the real, and the between.

You won't remember a lot. You might want to forget some things. You will remember things differently from each other, but it isn't a fight to see who remembers it best. Make sure you remember to make things up. Edit the stories into ones you can live.

As your GG told me when I was your age, There's no such thing really as Truth.

Live by the philosophy I grew up with:

Make-believe.
Make what you believe.
Believe in what you make.

I will leave things behind that you can keep if you need to, so when you sit on a chair, or open a book, or hold a blanket, it will be easy to conjure me up. But objects get lost, get broken, carry guilt. It's all too easy to build false shrines.

So please – forget inanimates. Seek sky. Seek land. Seek forest. Seek out the moon, and the night. I'll be there. Breathe me in deep.

Give away the objects. I don't need them. You don't either. But don't give away the puddles and trees. Gather seeds and scatter them in the ground. Forage. Pick the right mushrooms, like I showed you. Identify birds by their song. Name stars.

I need to write this here because maybe, when it's useful, my brain or my mouth won't work. Or these stories will come spilling out of me like nonsense and they'll call it dementia and you'll wonder what's truth. Because by then it will be hard to riddle and unriddle it, and you will wish later you had written the essence of these things down.

You can make things up. We all do. How else could we keep living with so much unknown. We all have to write ourselves into things. It makes us feel a little less alone. It doesn't matter if it's accurate. Like Shakespeare. *The brightest heaven of invention.* It only matters if it feels true to you.

I am writing this because one of you is fact and one imagination. This book can be the leaf stem to give you symmetry. Neither is right or better than the other. You need each other to complete the whole.

We are molecules and memories. We are stories and cells. We are love, chemical love in a diagram, as well as a love we cannot fathom or name. Know this: there are many routes to loving. It doesn't matter how you get there, but do. It is an act of noticing. That's all. Of seeing something or someone in the way they deserve. Let yourself notice things with the whole of you, as you do now. It is easy to grow up and forget that skill.

What I am saying is – one day, my loves, you will be here and I, my loves, will not.

It will always be a breaking, messy world. It takes time to trust your own dust. But I love your dust, every little speck of it, and we will pour our dust into each other, for as long as we can.

There is nothing more important and more urgent than this: one day, you will let me go to the earth, my loves, and I don't want there to be anything you don't know.

And This Too Is True –

– that I am grateful. I am grateful. For everyone, and everything, in this odd little world. I'm alive. We're alive. And it's beautiful, for a moment, to sweep the dust we share into a book.

To my family, to my women, to my children. To friendship: to Sol and Sam and Simon, to Lori and Laura and Lucie and more. To Thor (I love you, dickhead). To my sisterhood of students, who teach me more than I them. To Melissa, for lifting me, always. To Jamie and Silvie, who gave hope a pulse, and all at Canongate who got the blood flowing through.

To my coven of female writers, who wrote the *I* before my *I* began. Who put an *I* on the page for all women everywhere. Who breathed into I-hood the power of We-hood, holding us at times when it's impossible to go on. Chant their names, incant them:

> *Woolf and Plath and Paley, Lorde*
> *Angelou, Levy and Kay*
> *Ernaux, Cusk, Rich, Ditlevson*
> *Winterson, Shonagon, Gay*
> *Sexton, Sontag, Smith, Lispector, Cixous*
> *– too many to say*

(This is the kind of rhyme I make up to keep exercising, testing, my memory, my brain. Thanks, Brain, for putting up with me. I promise I'll be nicer to you from now on.)

★ ★ ★ ★

This part of a book is usually called Acknowledgements. *Acknowledgement*: (i) To notice someone or something; (ii) To recognise importance; (iii) To confirm receipt; (iv) *The acceptance of the truth or existence of something.* Etymology: Old English, 'to know'.

So – let's notice each other. Recognise importance. Confirm receipt of everything, good and bad, sent our way. Accept each other's truth and existence. Know each other, knowably and nobly. Know ourselves and leave nothing unknown.